TOURING IN WINE COUNTRY

BURGUNDY

MITCHELL BEAZLEY

TOURING IN WINE COUNTRY
BURGUNDY

HUBRECHT DUIJKER

SERIES EDITOR
HUGH JOHNSON

Contents

**Touring in Wine Country
Burgundy**
by Hubrecht Duijker

First published in Great Britain in 1996
by Mitchell Beazley, an imprint of Reed
Consumer Books Limited, 25 Victoria
Street, London SW1H 0EX.

Reprinted 1997

Text copyright © Hubrecht Duijker 1996
Maps copyright © Reed Consumer
Books Limited 1996
All rights reserved

Text adapted in part from 'Burgundy – A
Wine Lover's Touring Guide' by Hubrecht
Duijker. First published 1993 by
Uitgeverij Het Spectrum BV.

No part of this publication may be repro-
duced or used in any form by any means,
electronic or mechanical, including photo-
copying, recording or by any information
storage and retrieval system, without
prior written permission of the publisher.

A CIP catalogue record of this book is
available from the British Library.

ISBN 1 85732 580 X

Editors: Susan Keevil, Lucy Bridgers
Art Editor: Paul Drayson
Cartographic Editor: Zoë Goodwin
Index: Angie Hipkin
Gazetteer: Sally Chorley
Production: Juliette Butler
Managing Editor: Sue Jamieson
Executive Art Editor: Susan Downing
Art Director: Gaye Allen
Cartography: Map Creation Limited
Illustrations: Polly Raines
Design: The Bridgewater Book Company

Typeset in Bembo and Gill Sans

Origination by
Mandarin Offset, Singapore

Printed and bound by
Toppan Printing Company, China

Foreword

Why is it that wine tasted in the cellar (or even in the region) of its birth has a magic, a vibrancy and vigour that makes it so memorable?

It is easy to think of physical reasons. The long journey to the supermarket shelf cannot be without some effect on a living creature - and wine is indeed alive, and correspondingly fragile.

It is even easier to think of romantic reasons: the power of association, the atmosphere and scents of the cellar, the enthusiasm of the grower as he moves from barrel to barrel...

No wonder wine touring is the first-choice holiday for so many people. It is incomparably the best way to understand wine - whether at the simple level of its scenery and culture, or deeper into the subtleties of its terroirs and the different philosophies of different producers.

There are armchair wine-books, coffee-table books, quick reference wine-books... even a pop-up wine book. Now with this series we have the wine-traveller's precise, pin-pointed practical guide to sleuthing through the regions that have most to offer, finding favourites and building up memories. The bottles you find yourself have the genie of experience in them.

Hugh Johnson

Introduction

To wine enthusiasts everywhere, the very name Burgundy is inextricably linked with some of the finest wines known throughout the world. Yet it is quite possible to pass through this region and not know that you have been in wine country at all – let alone in the most renowned wine region of France. The Paris-Lyon autoroute sails disdainfully from the hills of the Morvan over the vines of Beaune, then plunges on south following the plain of the Saône, with the vineyard-covered hills to the west scarcely noticeable.

Take time to come off the main road, though, and the treasures that have made Burgundy's wines so famed will be discovered. The workaday side of Burgundy can be seen in a thousand cellars, most small and cramped workshops rather than Médoc-style *chais*. For this is the domaine of the smallholder, proprietors owning just a hectare or two, and these often made up of ten or more tiny patches in as many different vineyards. To own ten hectares in Burgundy is to be a major figure in your village. In Bordeaux, such a holding would push a château well down the local pecking order (see page 12).

The region of Burgundy was once the richest of the ancient duchies in France, stretching right up through northern France into Flanders. The Hospices de Beaune, built in 1443 by Nicolas Rolin, chancellor to Philip the Good, is a fine example of the beautiful architecture reflecting this immense wealth. There is also a considerable amount of Flemish-style architecture throughout the region. Today it merely consists of just five *départements* in eastern France: Ain, Côte d'Or, Nièvre, Saône-et-Loire and Yonne, with the amount of land under vine a relatively modest 40,000 hectares, small compared with the 100,000 hectares or so belonging to

Bordeaux. The administrative capital of Burgundy is the city of Dijon, but its wine capital is Beaune. Lying halfway between Chablis to the north and Villefranche, the heart of Beaujolais, to the south, it is the logical base for a serious exploration of the area.

Left Harvesting at Corton-Charlemagne. Plastic trays are mainly used instead of these paniers; they are gentler on the grapes.

Above The enticing, old-fashioned style of St-Genioux de Sissoux is created by such small touches as this cheese list written in chalk.

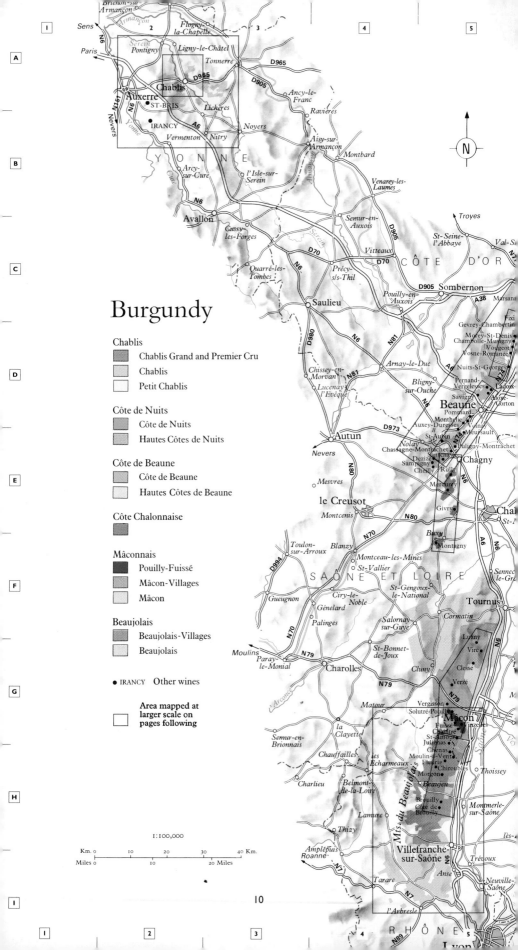

Right Relaxing and enjoying Burgundy's many liquid delights could not be easier with such a wide choice of bars and restaurants. Simply check the listings for the town or village you wish to visit.

THE REGIONS

Each of Burgundy's regions, from Chablis in the north to Beaujolais in the south, offers something different, not only in terms of wine, but also of landscape and culture.

The heart of Burgundy however, both historically and qualitively, is the Côte d'Or. Here, the most illustrious wines, both red and white, are produced. The vineyards trace the eastern slopes of a low, broad mountain chain in a southerly direction, almost all within the *département* of the same name. The exceptions are those vineyards with the appellation Maranges, in the extreme south of the Côte d'Or, which are situated in the Saône-et-Loire *département*.

From here it is only a few kilometres to the northern-most vineyards of the next district, the Chalonnais, or Côte Chalonnaise. The wines, red and white, tend to lack the complexity of Côte d'Or wines, but offer good value for money. Sparkling Crémant de Bourgogne is also made here.

The undulating landscape of the Chalonnais changes seamlessly into the Mâconnais, which is again dominated by hills and valleys, especially to the south where the landscape becomes quite dramatic. Mainly white wines are produced, including the Mâconnais' most famous, Pouilly-Fuissé.

Finally Beaujolais, the largest district, starts in the Saône-et-Loire and continues down to the *département* of Rhône, just north of Lyon. It is the most romantic Burgundian district; in some sleepy villages, time seems to have stood still. Your journey will then be complete, and some mysteries of this magical region uncovered.

Viticulture and Wines

Winegrowing in Burgundy is unusual as the scale is so small, with plots of vines often spread across several vineyards. The reasons are historical. After the French Revolution and subsequent breakdown of religious and secular rule, the land was shared out and further divided up by inheritance rights. Burgundy now has few estates larger than 25 hectares. This fragmentation is greatest in the Côte d'Or.

For many farmers, the lots are too small to make or bottle wine themselves. This is why the merchants, *négociants-éleveurs*, play such an important role in the Côte d'Or. They collect grapes, must or wine from small growers, assembling commercially viable quantities from single appellations.

In Chablis, the Chalonnais, Mâconnais and Beaujolais the emphasis shifts and *caves coopératives,* large groups of growers who pool their resources to make wines collectively, are common. In Mâconnais 90 percent of all wines are produced in this way and most of it is handled by *négociants*.

WINE CATEGORIES

Getting to grips with the French appellation system is hard enough, but in Burgundy it is particularly complicated. On the basis of the grape varieties used (see page 14) French law recognizes over 100 different appellations. They can be roughly divided into five categories:

Main picture *The harvest taking place in the Côte de Nuits, in this case, at the famous Domaine de la Romanée-Conti.*
Above *Removing particles in the wine (fining) by adding beaten egg whites. Bentonite clay is another substance useful for this process.*

Top right *During winter the vines are pruned and the unwanted canes are gathered and burned.*
Right *High-tech fermentation vats in Beaujolais.*

Regional/Generic Wine

Made throughout Burgundy: red and white burgundy, includes Bourgogne Aligoté, Bourgogne Passe-Tout-Grains and sparkling Crémant de Bourgogne.

District Wine

Can be made only in the (sub)districts concerned such as Chablis, Côte de Beaune-Villages, Mâcon and Beaujolais.

Village/Commune Wine

From a single commune or a group of communes: for example Gevrey-Chambertin (Côte d'Or), Pouilly-Fuissé (Mâconnais) and Fleurie (Beaujolais).

Premier Cru

Wines originating from a vineyard classed as Premier Cru. They are found in Chablis, the Côte d'Or and Chalonnais.

Grand Cru

The highest category. Grand Cru wines from the Côte d'Or are sold with the name of the vineyard alone – it has its very own appellation (Charmes-Chambertin, Corton-Charlemagne). Grand Cru wines from Chablis simply state Chablis Grand Cru along with the name of the vineyard.

CLIMATE AND SOIL

The soil throughout Burgundy has an enormous influence on the resulting wines and varies according to the region. In Chablis, limestone dominates and is well-suited to Chardonnay, as long as there is enough sun to ripen the grapes in these cool-climate vineyards. Add to this the variety of slopes – the Grand Cru vineyards are situated, some 150–200 metres high, on one stretch of southwest-facing slopes; most of the Premiers Crus face the other direction – it is easy to see how different the resulting wines can be.

The calcium-rich soil continues into the Côte d'Or but it becomes a more complex geology with layers of marl, clay and other soils present. Each soil-type influences factors such as drainage and soil temperature, affecting the ripening of grapes and ultimately the character of the wine itself. Limestone is still a feature of the Chalonnais, the Mâconnais and Beaujolais, but in this last region the soil can also be made up of decomposing slate. A subsoil of granite from ancient volcanoes also influences the flavour of these wines.

Climate has an enormous influence. From the northernmost vineyards of Chablis, it is about 300 kilometres to the southernmost point of Beaujolais. While Burgundy enjoys warm summers, it also suffers long, cold winters. Spring frosts and hail are a constant hazard, potentially devastating the crop. In Chablis, when frost threatens, heaters are often lit in the vineyards to warm the air above the vines. Sprinklers are also used to provide an insulating coating of ice that prevents the vines from freezing internally.

Travel south and the conditions become gradually milder. By the time you reach the Mâconnais there is already a slight Mediterranean touch to the air.

The grape varieties

O nly a few grape varieties are grown in Burgundy and they are rarely blended. There are four main varieties:

Chardonnay

This is one of the world's most noble white grapes. It may have originated from Burgundy itself and is responsible for the region's best white wines. It produces a firm, full wine and can have a range of flavours depending on how it is handled. In Burgundy, an elegant, minerally earthiness dominates the wines compared with the ripe tropical flavours found in the New World. The wines age well whether or not oak barrels were used during production.

Pinot Noir

The greatest red burgundy comes from Pinot Noir – the only red grape variety grown in the Côte d'Or. Compared with Chardonnay, it is more difficult to grow, requiring particular climatic conditions – fairly cool, yet warm enough to ripen the grapes. The wines are elegant and accessible, often easy to drink when young, but mature well. Soft red fruits and a silky texture are typical of good Pinot Noir and an earthy, gamey complexity is typical of good burgundy.

Left *The imposing product of a temperamental grape variety – red burgundy. Silky, reminiscent of soft red fruits and slightly gamey. Also very expensive to produce.*

Above *Chardonnay, the world's most famous grape variety, produces the region's finest white wines and the most sought after dry white wines in the world.*

Main picture *Pinot Noir grapes: difficult to ripen, susceptible to many diseases, but can produce exquisite, complex, long-living wines.*

Gamay

Gamay, (full name Gamay Noir à Jus Blanc) is the red Beaujolais grape, producing all the region's red or rosé wines, light, fresh, fruity and easy to drink. Most is made to be drunk young, but some of the serious Cru Beaujolais can age well, taking on a fuller, more complex style. Gamay is also produced in other parts of Burgundy, most notably in the Mâconnais. Bourgogne Passe-Tout-Grains also exists. This is made throughout Burgundy and is composed of two-thirds Gamay and a third Pinot Noir.

Aligoté

This white grape is made into Bourgogne Aligoté, formerly rather sour and meagre, but nowadays often succulent and fruity. Most comes from the area around Chablis, including Saint-Brix-le-Vineux and the Hautes-Côtes.

Other Varieties

Pinot Blanc (which can give surprisingly good wines here), the kindred Pinot Gris, Sauvignon Blanc (Sauvignon de St-Bris), Sacy and Melon de Bourgogne are present in limited quantities, as are César and Tressot.

Above *Gamay, the grape variety responsible for all red Beaujolais and also found in parts of Mâcon. Luscious sweet fruitiness is the hallmark of these wines.*

15

The cuisine

The people of Burgundy love the good life and always sit down to eat with the greatest of pleasure, whether at home or in a restaurant. Hundreds of restaurants flourish in this region and while some are luxurious and exclusive the majority are simple and frequently used by the locals. A three or four course menu can, therefore, be surprisingly inexpensive. Away from the major tourist attractions, such as the centre of Beaune, menu prices are usually only about FF100, and sometimes even less than this.

Specialities
Traditional Burgundian recipes have been handed down from generation to generation, most of them making full use of the many fresh ingredients produced in the region, such as the famous beef from the white Charolais cattle, the raw hams from Morvan, crayfish, many types of salt-water fish, snails, mustard (from Dijon) and a large range of cheeses. Goats' cheese plays a particularly important role in the Mâconnais and Beaujolais and there are numerous versions to choose from. There is also a delicious variety called Montrachet and a delectable caraway cheese called Epoisses, which is sprinkled with the local spirit Marc de Bourgogne. What is interesting, especially to the red-wine-with-cheese traditionalist, is that white burgundy often tastes just as good (and sometimes even better) drunk with the regional cheeses as red burgundy does.

Throughout Burgundy a lot of vegetables and fruit are grown and soft fruits such as blackberries, raspberries and

Far left *Garlic, one of the most vivid images of Burgundian cuisine and, indeed, of France as a whole.* Left *Crème de Cassis, made in many villages in Burgundy, is the key ingredient for the popular blackcurrant-flavoured drink, Kir.*

cherries are widespread. Many Burgundian winemakers also make the fruit liqueurs Crème de Cassis and Crème de Framboise, which, when mixed with white (and sometimes red) wine create the delicious apéritif Kir.

On the basis of the ingredients just mentioned, the Burgundian chefs prepare local specialities which taste just as marvellous as the accompanying wines. These include the delicious cheese canapés *gougères,* nutritious and wholesome *salade Beaujolaise* with chicken livers and bacon, *oeufs en meurette* (poached eggs in red wine sauce), frog's legs, *jambon persillé* (chunky pieces of ham in a white wine jelly with parsley and garlic), *escargots de Bourgogne* (snails with garlic) and *andouillettes,* sausages for which numerous regional recipes exist. There are just as many variations of *coq au vin,* if only because of the numerous different types of wine. In every village in Beaujolais this dish is prepared with the local wine. *Poulet* or *volaille de Bresse* often appears *à la crème* on the menu, with or without *morilles* mushrooms. *Boeuf à la bourguigonne* or *boeuf bourguignon,* which is served in count-less restaurants, is beef cooked in red wine, with onion, pieces of bacon and mushrooms. *Jambon à la lie de vin* is ham braised in the wine lees (sediment) produced during fer-mentation. *Lapin rôti* (roast rabbit) is also a traditional dish, often with a mustard and cream sauce. *Rable de lièvre* (saddle of hare) and many types of game, including *sanglier* and *marcassin* (wild boar and young wild boar respectively) are fairly common and ideal served with red wines from the Côte d'Or. The excellent beef from Charolais is frequently served as sirloin steaks with marrow and wine sauce. Blackberries and the liqueur made from them (Crème de Mûre) are often used in desserts such as sorbets and pies. Those who enjoy Burgundian cui-sine and wines understand why the French critic Curnonsky described this area as 'a gastronomic paradise'.

Above *Goats' cheese, found in many different forms throughout Burgundy and perfect with the region's wines.*
Left *Snails – one of Burgundy's most famous delicacies, often served as a starter, drenched with garlic-butter and herbs.*

How to use this guide

Above *An entrance to a vineyard in Mercurey, Côte Chalonnaise (see page 96) – a commune which produces a rich, supple red wine with good structure and a tiny amount of delicate white wine.*

This guide leads you through the length of Burgundy, starting in Chablis in the north and working its way southwards through the Côte d'Or, Chalonnais and Mâconnais to Beaujolais. Wine routes are suggested within each region, taking in every important wine village. Other places of interest are included, as well as suggested detours, scenic routes, views and walks. Hotels and restaurants are recommended, all with prices (hotel prices are usually for a double room). Some of the best and most welcoming wine producers or *négociant* firms are recommended for each village, often with the names of their best wines.

HOTELS

When reserving a hotel room always ask for a quiet one and watch out for loud church bells and popular, noisy cafés or bars. When making your reservation you will be informed of a final arrival time. If you intend to arrive later, telephone them, or your room may be given away. It is wise to send or

fax written confirmation of a reservation. In many villages (such as in Hautes-Côtes de Nuits) rooms in private houses are available, look for the signs *gîte* or *chambre d'hôte* or consult the list of addresses at the town hall or at the *syndicat d'initiative* (tourist office).

RESTAURANTS

Telephone restaurants in advance to be sure of a table, and to check that it is open on that particular day. Off season, many restaurants are open only three or four days a week.

Fixed menus often offer the best value for money and use the freshest produce of the day. In simple restaurants choose regional dishes, they will be better prepared and less expensive. Select regional wines and if possible wines from the village itself, as they will have been more expertly and critically chosen. A carafe of tap water is always free.

WINEGROWERS

It maybe difficult to get an appointment to see the most famous winegrowers, but the less well-known will generally welcome you with pleasure. Do not hesitate to show them this guide: someone who comes by recommendation and is truly interested in wines is usually more pleasantly received than a passing stranger. When tasting the wines it is normal to spit them out, but first ask where you can do this. Never tip but buy at least one bottle of their wine as a token of appreciation (this is unnecessary if you have paid for the visit). French is generally the only language spoken, although many young winegrowers nowadays speak English.

CHOOSING WINES TO BUY

Choosing the best wines to buy in Burgundy is not easy given the number of growers and *négociants*. Price need not reflect quality, nor even the appellation. Widely varying wines can be produced from grapes grown in the same vineyard but by different owners. As winemaking methods also vary, so does the quality of the wine. Repute counts more than price or appellation.

PLACES OF INTEREST

Burgundy is steeped in history and cultural interest. Details of the most interesting places are included.

MAPS

Detailed wine maps showing commune appellation boundaries, Grands and Premiers Crus, and other vineyard boundaries are included, with suggested wine routes. These routes take in the most important villages and vineyards, but if you have time to explore further then so much the better.

Chablis

The first great Burgundian vineyards you reach when driving south from Paris are those of Chablis in the Yonne *département*.

It is only through historical coincidence that Chablis belongs to Burgundy (it was absorbed into the Duchy of Burgundy in 1477), because its location, climate and soil all suggest it could just as well belong to Champagne. The best vineyards of Chablis, like those of Champagne, contain a lot of limestone. In Chablis the thick lime layer was formed by the fossils of countless shellfish, usually small oysters with a comma-like shell. The soil is *Kimméridgian*, named after Kimmeridge on the south coast of England, because a similar limestone layer is found there. It is the lime that that is believed to give the wines of Chablis, exclusively white, their distinctive austere character. Wines made from Chardonnay are characterized by a pale colour, often with a green tinge, and a very dry, somewhat mineral-like, cool taste which can be succulent and fruity at the same time.

There are four categories of Chablis. The best wines, the Grands Crus, come from seven slopes directly to the north of Chablis: Blanchots, Bougros, Les Clos, Grenouilles, Les Preuses, Valmur and Vaudésir. They offer intense flavours, full of strength and character and are at their best a few years after bottling. Somewhat lighter and less pronounced in character, but still with a marked identity, are the wines from the Premier Cru sites. These come from some 580 hectares divided between 30 different vineyards. Wines from these vineyards may be sold under the name of the individual vineyard, or under the name of a group of vineyards, the latter being more common.

Left The soft, undulating lines of the Chablis landscape with the pale Kimméridgian soil that gives the wines such distinctive character.

Above This sign is typical of those used to indicate a winemaking domaine. Most producers are clearly signposted in this way.

Chablis

- –·––·–– Arrondissement boundary
- ––––·––– Canton boundary
- –––––––– Commune (parish) boundary

LES CLOS

- Chablis Grand Cru
- Chablis Premier Cru
  (BEAUROY : new name, Troësmes : old name)
- Chablis
- Woods
- —50— Contour interval 10 metres
- Wine route

1:50,000

Km. 0 ———— 1 ———— 2 Km.
Miles 0 ———— 1 Mile

Below Michel Martin is one of the producers in Coulanges-la-Vineuse, a village making red burgundy.

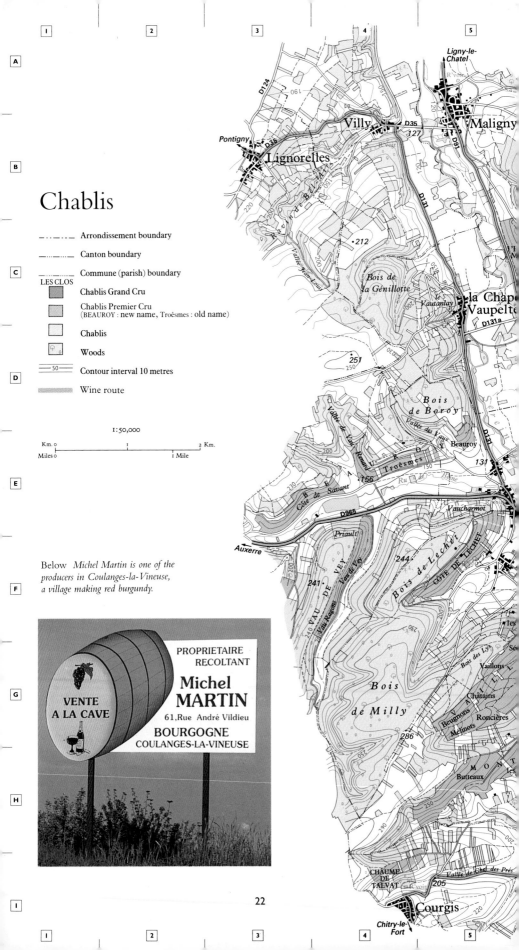

22

By far the largest number of wines are sold as straight-forward Chablis; in fact, twice as much wine is made from grapes grown outside the Grand Cru and Premier Cru vine-yards. Quality can vary greatly, from fruity and clean to flat and aggressive; disappointing, especially considering the high prices Chablis often demands. Finally there is Petit Chablis, a wine which is increasingly modest, both in quan-tity and quality, and in which the characteristics of a true Chablis are hard to find.

CHABLIS AND ITS IMMEDIATE AREA

The town of Chablis itself is 12 kilometres from the A6 Autoroute du Soleil (exit Auxerre-Sud). The winding road runs through Beines which has an ancient medieval church. On the north side is a large man-made lake which protects the surrounding vineyards against night-time frosts by retaining

Right Gougères, *cheese-flavoured choux pastry puffs, are often served with wine throughout Burgundy.*

CHABLIS

HOTELS

Hôtel de l'Etoile
Tel: 86 42 10 50
Fairly basic rooms (14) starting at about FF300. In the restaurant you can eat inexpensively (menus from around FF120). Wide choice of local wines, also older wines. Situated near the central square.

Hostellerie des Clos
Tel: 86 42 10 63
The best hotel and restaurant of the district. Rooms start at around FF250. In the light, large dining room, you can eat very well. The least expensive set menu (around FF165) offers particularly good value for money. Wide wine selection. The owner, Michel Vignaud, is the cook.

Les Lys
Tel: 86 42 49 20
Functional, two-star hotel in south Chablis. Around 40 modern rooms starting at about FF225.

Le Relais Saint-Vincent
Tel: 86 47 53 38
Peaceful, small hotel at Ligny-le-Châtel; attractive rooms (10) starting at FF200. Also has a restaurant.

RESTAURANTS

Auberge du Bief
Tel: 86 47 43 42
At Ligny-le-Châtel, on a corner, near the church on the river-bank. Traditional local dishes as well as more refined cuisine. Popular with the locals. Menus start at FF155.

Le Syracuse
Tel: 86 42 19 45
Inexpensive and tasty regional dishes, for example *andouillettes grillées*, (made by the butcher next door) and *coq au St-Bris*. Large wine list. Situated on the village square.

Le Vieux Moulin
Tel: 86 42 47 30
This restaurant is located in an old watermill (Rue des Moulins, across from the l'Obédiencerie). Regional cuisine, also *grillades*. Good wine list, reasonable prices (menus starting at FF100). Part of the Les Lys hotel.

Au Vrai Chablis
Tel: 86 42 11 43
A bar and restaurant on the village square. You can eat well here for FF100 and less. Tasty salads.

some warmth from the sun's rays after dark – this, in effect, creates a warmer microclimate by warming the air around the lake and preventing the dramatic night-time temperature fluctuations which can cause such severe frosts.

Chablis itself is a small, quiet town, built around a main square. To the north of this square is the Romanesque-Gothic church of Saint-Martin. The heavy large wooden doors at the southern entrance of the church are covered with horseshoes, nailed on as offerings by pilgrims asking the saint to revive their tired horses.

The Serein River flows along the northeastern side of Chablis. In an old street, the Rue des Moulins, you will find l'Obédiencerie, a 15th-century building originally belonging to monks, that has an ancient wooden wine press. The building is now owned by the large Chablis producer, Domaine Laroche (visits by appointment).

Otherwise, Chablis doesn't have many old streets, because it was badly damaged by bombs during the second world war. However, the towers of the Porte Noël are reminders of a time when Chablis was walled and, thanks to the wine production, considerably prosperous. In the southern part of the town is the 12th-century church of Saint-Pierre, which is classified as a historic monument.

An unmissable sight is the fantastic view from the Panorama des Clos. Cross the Serein River to the east bank and follow the road straight on to the T-junction. Turn right here onto the D965 and take the first left. Climb uphill past the Grand Cru vineyards on your left until you reach the view-point from the woods.

Unlike other wine regions of France, Chablis does not have a signposted wine route, but the following will provide a good introduction to the area.

From the centre of Chablis, cross the Serein to the east bank and turn left onto the D91 going north along the river bank towards Maligny. On the slopes to the right are the best vineyards of the district, the Grands Crus. You may want to make a small diversion by turning right onto the D216 to Fontenay-près-Chablis to see the 11th-century church there. Return to the D91 and drive for about seven kilometres to the village of Maligny. On the way you pass, to the left, the water pump station which plays an invaluable role when frost is a danger to crops (see page 13). The stretch of vineyard on the right is the Premier Cru of Fourchaume.

In Maligny itself is the château, situated in a large park, and currently being lovingly restored by winegrower Jean Durup. In the centre, by an old market hall, is the medieval church of Notre-Dame which is worth a visit.

Another 3.5 kilometres along the D91 is Ligny-le-Châtel, with striking church featuring a Romanesque nave, a Renaissance-style chancel and many religious works of art. The road takes you back across the River Serein. Take the first turning left to Pontigny to visit its famous 12th- to 13th-century monastery. This was the largest Cistercian church of its time in France and one of the first Gothic buildings in Burgundy. Thanks to these monks, winegrowing around Chablis flourished as long ago as the Middle Ages.

RECOMMENDED PRODUCERS

Billaud-Simon (Chablis)
Important estate owning many vineyards on the sought-after right bank of the Serein River, including plots in four Grands Crus. Technically very sophisticated.

La Chablisienne (Chablis)
Large cooperative with about 280 members. The wines are of reliable quality and are usually good value.

Domaine du Chardonnay (Chablis)
Established in 1987 by three young growers. Reliable, fruity wines: Petit Chablis, Chablis and Chablis Premiers Crus.

René et Vincent Dauvissat (Chablis)
Traditional estate producing delicious wines, among the best of the district. The range includes two Grands Crus and three Premiers Crus.

Jean-Paul Droin (Chablis)
This company produces more than ten types of Chablis, almost all of good to excellent quality. The four Grands Crus are particularly worth trying.

Domaine de l'Eglantière (Maligny)
The largest private wine estate in Chablis, founded by the dynamic Jean Durup. The wines – in particular Chablis and Premiers Crus – are of excellent quality despite the large volumes produced.

Domaine Corinne et Jean-Pierre Grossot (Chablis)
Specializes in ordinary Chablis, but also makes some excellent Premiers Crus, among them Vaucoupin, Mont de Milieu, Fourchaume and Côte de Troêsmes.

Domaine Laroche (Chablis)
This estate owns a fine tasting centre in Chablis itself, and the old l'Obédiencerie building. The wines are made in a modern complex south of Chablis. Expensive but of consistently high quality and simply labelled 'Laroche'.

Domaine Long Depaquit (Chablis)
This once-renowned estate of some 50 hectares belongs to the Albert Bichot firm at Beaune. It seems gradually to be regaining something of its former glory.

Left Intricate ironwork on a wine-producer's gateway in Chablis. For centuries, wine production has been a great source of wealth for the region, which details like this reflect.

Right Chablis was badly bombed during the war, but by the Serein River in the centre of the town, remain several historical buildings.

Domaine de la Maladière (Chablis)

A high profile domaine with a large range of excellent wines. The best are fermented and matured in oak casks. The proprietor, William Fevre, owns more Grands Crus than anyone in Chablis with 15% of the total and vines in every one except Blanchots. He does, however, buy grapes from there as well so that he can offer wines from all of them.

Domaine des Malandes (Chablis)

Memorable, high-quality wines, fermented and aged in tank, not oak. Among the best are the Premiers Crus Côte de Lechet, Fourchaume, Montmains, Vau de Vey and the Grands Crus Les Clos and Vaudésir.

Louis Michel & Fils (Chablis)

Old family estate offering fresh, complex, unwooded wines which age wonderfully well. You can taste them in the 17th-century cellar.

J Moreau & Fils (Chablis)

Large company with about 85 hectares, of which 25 are Grands and Premiers Crus. Christian Moreau opposes the use of oak for any Chablis as he believes it does not suit the mineral character of the wine.

Domaine Gilbert Picq et Ses Fils (Chichée)

A rising star. The Chablis Vieilles Vignes has class.

Domaine Pinson (Chablis)

Traditional methods are followed here. Thus the wines are matured in wooden casks. Wonderful, quite full Les Clos, and a similarly splendid Mont de Milieu.

François et Jean-Marie Ravenau (Chablis)

Distinguished wines with a steely coolness and fine complexity if allowed at least six years' bottle-age.

A Regnard & Fils (Chablis)

Property of Patrick de Ladoucette. This company produces fine, if rather expensive, wines.

Domaine Sainte Claire (Préhy)

Owned by Jean-Marc Brocard. Wines include the Premiers Crus Montmains, Vaillons, Vau Lignau, and the Grand Cru Valmur and all deserve attention.

Simonnet-Febvre (Chablis)

Small, serious company which acts as a broker for several merchants in Beaune. It also handles red and rosé Irancy wines.

Drive back to Chablis on the D131 towards Villy. Try to stop briefly in La Chapelle-Vaupelteigne in order to look at the old chapel and to enjoy the splendid view. In the next village, Poinchy, turn right onto the D965 to Milly. Here, there is a medieval chapel with a fine sculpture of a kneeling monk. The local château dates from the same period. The village of Milly is situated at foot of the Premier Cru vineyard, Côte de Léchet, and from the top of the vineyard there is a magnificent view over Chablis. Return via Poinchy, and turn right to get onto the D131 which takes you right back into Chablis itself.

To the south of Chablis the churches of Courgis and Préhy are worth a detour. Courgis, situated on a hill, also has interesting castle ruins, and from Préhy there is a fine view across the vineyards; look out for the village church which is surrounded by grape-vines.

AROUND CHABLIS – AUXERRE AND IRANCY

Just outside the district of Chablis in the Auxerrois region, there are four principal communes: Saint-Bris-le-Vineux, Chitry, Irancy and Coulanges-la-Vineuse, the first two producing mainly white wines (Crémant de Bourgogne and Bourgogne Aligoté) and the latter two mainly reds.

The most important wine municipality is Saint-Bris-le-Vineux where the wine speciality is, rather surprisingly, Sauvignon de Saint-Bris, a lively, aromatic wine made from the white grape variety Sauvignon Blanc. This grape has been growing here since the mid-19th century when it was used as part of a blend. Now it is vinified separately and has VDQS status. Sauvignon de Saint-Bris is often bought by wine-lovers in search of an alternative to the illustrious, more expensive Sauvignon wines from Sancerre and Pouilly Fumé: the wines are a little lighter in style.

Gérard Tremblay (Poinchy)
Modern cellars; fresh, clear-tasting wines such as Valmur Grand Cru and Fourchaume Premier Cru.
Domaine de Vauroux (Chablis) – Wines of character and quality.
Domaine Vocoret (Chablis)
Situated on the southern outskirts of Chablis. Large estate of about 40 hectares – four Grands Crus and various Premiers Crus. All the wines are currently fermented and aged in large wooden barrels.

WINE FESTIVAL

The annual Chablis wine festival takes place on the fourth Sunday of November.

AROUND CHABLIS

RESTAURANTS
Le Saint-Bris
Tel: 86 53 84 56
You can eat very well here for surprisingly little money. Even the Sunday à la carte menu costs less than FF85. At St-Bris-le-Vineux
Les Vendanges
Tel: 86 42 21 91
Simple village café and restaurant. For less than FF100 you can satisfy even the biggest hunger. It also has a few rooms. At Coulanges-la-Vineuse.

RECOMMENDED PRODUCERS
Caves de Bailly (St-Bris-le-Vineux)
Top quality white and rosé Crémant de Bourgogne are produced by modern methods here in vast underground cellars along the Yonne. These sparkling wines are the best of their kind.
Domaine Bersan & Fils
Large estate producing clean, usually aromatic wines, including the local Sauvignon, Bourgogne Aligoté and white burgundy. The ultra-modern cellar is situated outside the village of St-Bris.
Robert et Philippe Defrance
Fresh, fruity white wines.
Domaine Fort
Superior Sauvignon Blanc and attractive Irancy wines.
Ghislaine et Jean-Hugues Goisot
Charming, clean white wines.
Domaine des Remparts
Excellent wines.
Luc Sorin
Bourgogne Aligoté, Sauvignon de St-Bris and Bourgogne Irancy are produced and are all of high quality.

Right *Tending vines near Chablis. At times like this, viticulture appears barely different from other kinds of farming.*

From the village of Chablis, drive south on the D91 and turn right after only one kilometre onto the D62 to Courgis. Continue on through Chitry, which has a fortified church, to Saint-Bris-le-Vineux, a small village nestling on the side of a low hill. There are winegrowers' signs everywhere and many of them have fascinating ancient cellars dating from as far back as the 10th century. The local church, built in the 13th century, is particularly imposing.

Take time to visit the Caves de Bailly in the hamlet of Bailly, just outside Saint-Bris. This is an enormous cellar hewn out of a limestone quarry where thousands of bottles of the company's Crémant de Bourgogne are stored. It was stone from this quarry that was used to build the Panthéon in Paris, as well as many other notable buildings.

Below *The style of these tall gabled buildings in Auxerre's Place St-Nicholas reflect the northern location of the town itself.*

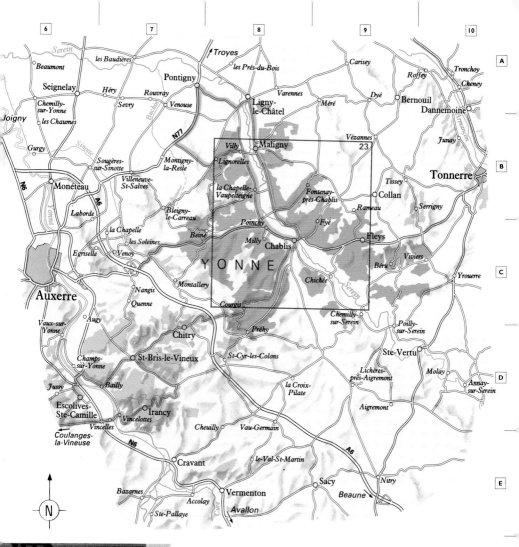

Around Chablis

Wine-producing areas

- Chablis
- Bourgogne Irancy
- Bourgogne
- Sauvignon-de-St-Bris

23 Area mapped at larger scale on page shown

Wine route

1:250,000

Km. 0 1 2 3 4 5 Km.
Miles 0 1 2 3 Miles

Above and right *Views of the town of Auxerre. This town produced much wine in the 18th and 19th centuries until phylloxera struck. Instead of replanting the vines, the town expanded.*
Far right *Irancy sits in one of France's most beautiful amphitheatres of vines, which also acts as a successful sun-trap.*

From Saint-Bris, take the D956 south, turning right at the signpost for Irancy after about one kilometre. The local wine, Bourgogne Irancy, is made from Pinot Noir but also contains a small amount of the little-known red grape César which, it is thought, may have originated here. The César contributes colour, tannin and backbone to the lighter Pinot-based wines, distinguishing Bourgogne Irancy from the mass of rather non-descript Bourgognes Rouges made all over the region.

Irancy sits at the very centre of a large amphitheatre of vineyards and is one of Burgundy's most beautifully located villages.

Continue straight on to Vincelottes, crossing the River Yonne there and driving straight on along the D85 to Coulanges-la-Vineuse. This village, situated on a hill and surrounding an eye-catching 18th-century church which has a tall, pointed tower, also produces light red wines, made entirely from Pinot Noir. The village has a small Musée de la Vigne; ask for admittance or make appointments either at the town hall or at the bar-restaurant Les Vendanges.

IRANCY

RECOMMENDED PRODUCERS

Léon Bienvenue
Leading grower who gives his red Bourgogne Irancy at least a year's ageing in cask.

Bernard Cantin
The mayor of Irancy and also producer of elegant, fruity wines.

René Charriat
Producer of a fairly light-coloured Irancy with a good level of alcohol.

Robert Colinot & Fils
This producer's red Irancy usually profits from a little bottle-age.

Roger Delalogue
Small grower with vaulted cellars where the red wines are kept in cask. Agreeable red and rosé Irancy for those who like light wines.

Jean Podor
Supple red Irancy. It has some depth in warm, sunny years.

COULANGES-LA-VINEUSE

RECOMMENDED PRODUCERS

Raymond Dupuis
One of the district's best growers. The red wine has fruit and charm and is reasonably rounded.

André Martin & Fils
If the sun cooperates, the red wine from this estate has the backbone to age for some years.

WINE FESTIVAL

On the weekend before November 11th, St-Bris-le-Vineux usually celebrates the Fête du Sauvignon.

The Côte d'Or

The Côte d'Or is the heart of Burgundy. It lies along the irregular hillside which starts just south of Dijon and stretches for 50 kilometres in a southwesterly direction, ending at Santenay. Almost the entire wine area is situated within the *département* of the same name; only a few communes in the extreme south, under the appellation of Maranges, belong to a different *département*, Saône-et-Loire.

The wine villages and their vineyards lie along the *route nationale* 74 (RN 74), which runs straight down through the Côte d'Or connecting Dijon with Chagny. It is a busy road which is sometimes difficult to avoid, but if you have the time, do try to take the smaller roads. In the north for example, between Marsannay and Nuits-Saint-Georges, you can follow a peaceful parallel route to the west of the *route nationale*, which runs through some of the most famous wine villages. A similar road runs further south between the villages of Pommard and Santenay.

The best vineyards are situated on the well-exposed, east-facing slopes conveniently sheltered from westerly rain-bearing winds by the wooded escarpment that runs above them. The soil here is so diverse that often even neighbouring vineyards will have quite different soil characteristics. Added to this, the land is divided up into extremely small plots each owned by different growers. The result is that burgundy is produced by lots of growers, each making small amounts of a wide range of different wines. The quantities are often so small that it makes little sense for the growers to try to sell the wines themselves, which is why the shippers, the *négociants-éleveurs*, play such an important role. They buy these small parcels of wine, blend them and sell them under their own label. Some growers do bottle and sell their own wines and many have received international acclaim, consequently charging high prices that reflect this.

To make matters even more complicated, the quality of wine made by the growers varies quite considerably, even in the same year. It is, therefore, important to know the reputation of the winemaker rather than banking simply on the classification of the vineyard. A 'village' wine bearing just the name of its commune, but from a quality-conscious

Left Beaune's Hôtel Dieu with its traditional coloured-tile roof, built by Nicolas Rollin in 1443.

Above Vineyards in Chambolle-Musigny, a commune producing a light, fragrant style of wine.

grower, may be better than a Premier Cru from a lax estate. The wines of the Côte d'Or are divided into four classes. The top category is **Grand Cru**, which applies to 30 individual vineyards, including Chambertin, Musigny, Clos de Vougeot and Montrachet. Wines made from these vineyards are sold under the vineyard name, with no mention of the commune they are situated in.

The next class is **Premier Cru** which includes over 300 of the best vineyards. Premier Cru wines are sold with the name of the relevant commune and the name of the vineyard, or simply the words Premier Cru if the wine is a blend of grapes from more than one vineyard.

The third class is that of **village** or **commune** appellation such as Gevrey-Chambertin. These wines can be sold with their vineyard names appearing in smaller type along with the name of the commune. This category includes the *Côtes de Nuits* villages and *Côtes de Beaune* villages appellations.

The fourth category includes **regional** wines – the Bourgogne, Bourgogne Aligoté etc. These wines often come from the flatter land to the east of the RN74. Also worth investigating are the wines from the hilly areas to the west of the Côte d'Or – the Hautes-

Above *A traditional* panier *used by grape-pickers here at the Romanée-Conti, with an essential pair of secateurs to remove the bunches from the vine.*

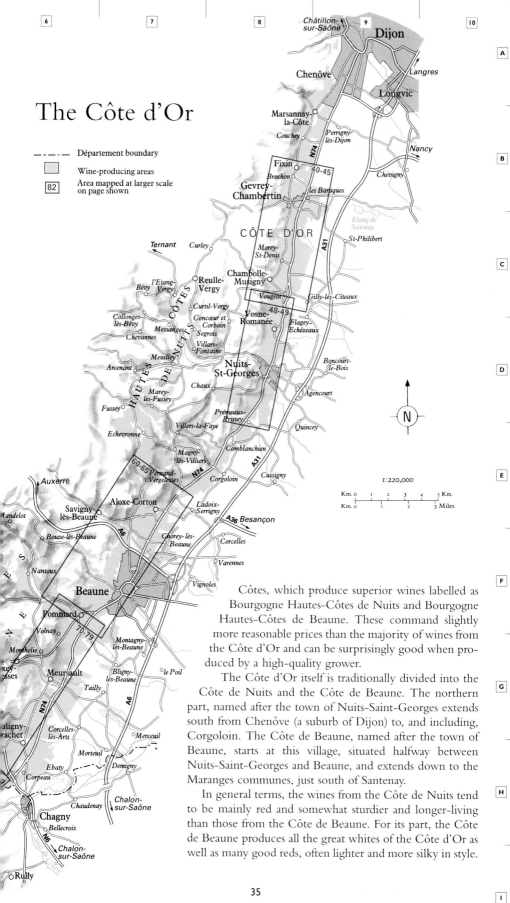

The Côte d'Or

- – · – · – Département boundary
- ▢ Wine-producing areas
- ▢82 Area mapped at larger scale on page shown

CÔTE D'OR

HAUTES-CÔTES DE NUITS

Côtes, which produce superior wines labelled as Bourgogne Hautes-Côtes de Nuits and Bourgogne Hautes-Côtes de Beaune. These command slightly more reasonable prices than the majority of wines from the Côte d'Or and can be surprisingly good when produced by a high-quality grower.

The Côte d'Or itself is traditionally divided into the Côte de Nuits and the Côte de Beaune. The northern part, named after the town of Nuits-Saint-Georges extends south from Chenôve (a suburb of Dijon) to, and including, Corgoloin. The Côte de Beaune, named after the town of Beaune, starts at this village, situated halfway between Nuits-Saint-Georges and Beaune, and extends down to the Maranges communes, just south of Santenay.

In general terms, the wines from the Côte de Nuits tend to be mainly red and somewhat sturdier and longer-living than those from the Côte de Beaune. For its part, the Côte de Beaune produces all the great whites of the Côte d'Or as well as many good reds, often lighter and more silky in style.

DIJON

HOTELS

Wilson
Place Wilson
Tel: 80 66 82 50
This hotel, built in the 17th century
as a coaching inn, has comfortable
rooms from around FF400. See
restaurant Thibert.

Chapeau Rouge
5 Rue Michelet
Tel: 80 30 28 10
Luxurious hotel with highly rated
restaurant (one Michelin star). Rooms
from around FF650.

Parc de la Colombière
49 Cours Parc
Tel: 80 65 18 41
Rooms starting at around FF300.
Pleasant outdoor seating area.

Dijon

The most direct route from Chablis to Dijon is to return to the A6 motorway from Chablis and, heading south for approximately 100 kilometres, leave the motorway at Pouilly-en-Auxois and take the A38 east to Dijon. For those with more time to amble across the countryside, there is a more scenic route: from Chablis, take the D965 to Tonnerre and then turn south onto the D905. This road meanders along the Armançon River to Montbard then along the River Brenne before joining the A38 just outside Dijon. Turn left onto the A38 heading east into the town centre. From Tonnerre to the A38 is about 130 kilometres.

Despite having somewhat unattractive suburbs, the centre of Dijon is still very pretty. After a large fire in the 12th-century it was rebuilt by the Burgundian Duke Hugo II and

Dijon's rich heritage makes it a great stopping-off point en route to the vineyards further south, for antiques shopping (top) or simply admiring the architecture (above).

Above left *Rue de la Liberté, and left, Rue Verrière: Timbered buildings in the city centre are a reminder of Dijon's prosperous past.*

remains of this period can still be found. Dijon's greatest days of prosperity, however, were between 1364 and 1477, when four successive dukes of Valois – one of whom was Philip the Bold – turned the city, politically and culturally, into one of the most important centres of Europe.

There was a second affluent period between the 16th and 18th centuries. The princes of Condé were the governers and prosperous citizens enriched Dijon with marvellous buildings.

Religion has always been important in this city with at least six churches in the city centre. The cathedral of Saint-Bénigne is the oldest. Its crypt dates from the 11th century and the rest of the architecture is mainly 13th century. Dijon has eight museums, one of which – the archeological museum – is situated in the former monastery buildings, by the cathedral.

Also notable is the Gothic Notre-Dame which has a wonderful façade. Inside there is, among other artefacts, a 12th-century wooden Black Virgin statue. The church of Saint-Michel, on the same square, is also worth a visit.

The most beautiful parts of the city are found in the walks between the churches. The pedestrianized Rue de la Liberté is the most important shopping street with its half-timbered houses and cafés where you can sit and simply watch the world go by. The role of wine in the region is reflected in the Place François Rude whose fountain is decorated with a figure treading grapes. Leading off this is the Rue des Forges, full of beautiful houses, all reflecting the prosperity of the town. Further riches can be found at the Place de la Libération where the impressive Palace of the Dukes of Burgundy and the States General of Burgundy is situated. The building now houses the town hall and the Museum for Fine Arts, which is regarded by many as the best art gallery in France outside Paris.

Also near here is the Musée François Rude where you can admire works by the sculptor Rude who was born in Dijon. This museum is situated in part of the former abbey of St-Etienne (not far from the previously mentioned church of Saint-Michel).

If you really fall under the spell of the venerable riches of Dijon, then you can also dine in an historic ambiance, because at 18 Rue Sainte-Anne is the restaurant La Toison d'Or, which has a small museum. The collection includes ancient wine utensils as well as scenes from French history recreated with models. What's more, the food is delicious (menus starting at about FF140, Tel: 80 30 73 52).

Below Pain d'épices *(spiced bread), often made with honey and highly popular throughout France.*

RESTAURANTS

Thibert
10 Place Wilson
Tel: 80 67 74 64
This highly rated restaurant is part of the Hôtel Wilson. The cooking is of a high standard and the wine list is comprehensive. Menus start at FF200. Closed August 1 to 23.

Jean-Pierre Billoux
Hôtel la Cloche, 14 Place Darcy
Tel: 80 30 11 00
Another of Dijon's highly rated restaurants with impeccably prepared dishes and an extensive wine list (good selection of local wines). Menus start at around FF250. Closed August 8 to 17.

La Dame d'Aquitaine
23 Place Bossuet
Tel: 80 30 36 23
Quaintly located restaurant in a 13th-century crypt. Menus start at around FF130. Restaurant is closed on Sundays and Monday lunchtimes.

La Côte St-Jean
13 Rue Monge
Tel: 80 50 11 77
Pleasant, reasonably priced restaurant with menus starting at around FF90. Closed July 24 to August 7, and on Tuesdays and Saturday lunchtimes.

The Côte de Nuits

The Côte de Nuits stretches from Marsannay down to Corgoloin. This part of the Côte d'Or is red wine country; white is a rarity here. At the northern end of the Côte de Nuits the firmest, longest-living and eventually most velvety red bugundies are made. Time is rewarded by complex elegant wines, with an incredible depth of flavour.

Leaving Dijon from the south of the city, travel south on the N74 towards Chenôve. Legend has it that, in 1648, the wines of Chenôve fetched higher prices than those of Gevrey, perhaps partly because of the famous Clos du Roi vineyard which was owned by the Duke of Burgundy.

From Chenôve, instead of returning to the busy N74, take the D122 Route des Grands Crus which runs in a southerly direction just west of the N74 and parallel to it. This winds a much more peaceful and scenic route through the villages between Chenôve and Nuits-Saint-Georges.

MARSANNAY-LA-COTE

Like Chenôve, Marsannay-la-Côte has become a commuter town because of its proximity to Dijon. It has lost many of its vineyards, although vines still cover a fifth of the land.

The tiny town centre is worth a stop for refreshments and some fresher air after Dijon's busy city centre. There are two bars in the church square where you can quench your thirst, Café de la Place owned by Christian Bouvier and Café des Sports, also known locally as 'Chez Marianne'.

Here, and in the local restaurants, you can savour the most famous rosé of Burgundy, Rosé de Marsannay. The wine, first made by Joseph Clair in 1919, is made from vinifying Pinot Noir grapes as if they were white. The last pressings produce a pink-tinged juice which gives the wine its pink-grey colour. However, the village was granted its own

Left *The Clos de Vougeot. The monks of Cîteaux wisely divided it into three cuvées according to the* quality of the soil. The Cuvées: des Papes (upper part), des Rois (the middle) and des Moines (bottom).

appellation for red and white wines in 1987 which may result in less rosé being made in the future. Even now, the accent is really on red wine which accounts for three times the volume of rosé.

FIXIN

The charming village of Fixin is situated just three kilometres south of Marsannay on the D122 Route des Grands Crus. Before Marsannay acquired its own appellation, Fixin was the first appellation contrôlée south of Dijon. This is the beginning of the *vrai* Côte de Nuits – mainly concentrated red wines benefiting from some years of bottle age.

Formerly called Fiscentix, the dukes of Burgundy had a summer residence here with its own vineyard. The 12th-century hunting lodge, later given to the monks of Cîteaux, still exists and is now a wine estate, the Clos de la Perrière, and is Fixin's most famous Premier Cru vineyard.

Right next to the Clos de la Perrière is Fixin's other Premier Cru vineyard, Clos du Chapître. Also notable is the Clos Napoléon, which borders the Parc Noisot. Situated against a wooded hill above Fixin, these gardens were created in 1837 by Claude Noisot, an old commandant of the imperial guard, in hommage to Napoléon. A replica of the house in which the exiled emperor lived on Saint-Helena was built and this now houses Napoleonic memorabilia.

Fixin and the neighbouring hamlet of Fixey have beautiful churches with the traditional multicoloured spires. There is also a small museum of wine artefacts in the 17th-century cellar of Domaine du Clos St-Louis.

Above *The Grand Cru Latricières Chambertin: an extremely elegant and lacy wine, as its name suggests.*

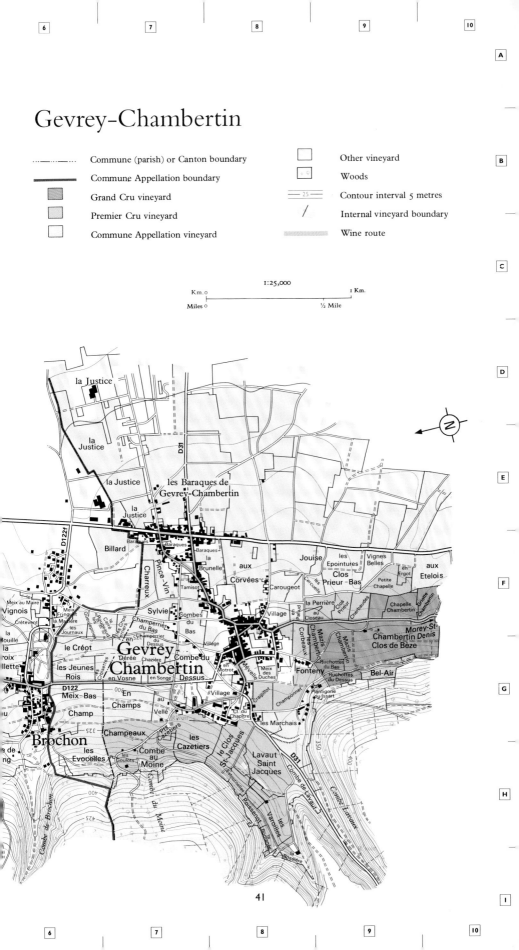

Gevrey-Chambertin

Commune (parish) or Canton boundary
Commune Appellation boundary
Grand Cru vineyard
Premier Cru vineyard
Commune Appellation vineyard

Other vineyard
Woods
Contour interval 5 metres
Internal vineyard boundary
Wine route

1:25,000

Km. 0 — 1 Km.
Miles 0 — ½ Mile

MARSANNAY

RESTAURANTS

Des Gourmets
Tel: 80 52 16 32
Celebrated, busy restaurant. Varied
wine list. Menus start at about FF180.
La Renardière
Tel: 80 52 16 41
Regional dishes. Menus under FF100.

RECOMMENDED PRODUCERS

Domaine Charlopin-Parizot
Good, notable wines.
Bruno Clair Four delicious Rosés
de Marsannay produced. Traditional
reds are admirable.
Domaine Huguenot Père & Fils
Decent, slightly oaked, intense
burgundies. Also a pleasant rosé.

FIXIN

HOTEL

**Domaine de Saint-Antoine
Fixey**
Tel: 80 52 46 16
Peacefully situated hotel. Six
rooms. Prices about FF300.

RESTAURANT

Chez Jeanette
Tel: 80 52 45 49
Regional dishes. Three set menus
under FF150. Also has rooms.

RECOMMENDED PRODUCERS

Vincent et Denis Berthaut
Traditional wines needing age. The
best are the Fixin Premier Crus.
Jacques Durand-Roblot Rustic
and reliable wines.
Domaine Pierre Gelin Solid reds,
more rustic than sophisticated.

GEVREY-CHAMBERTIN

HOTEL

Les Grands Crus
Tel: 80 34 34 15
Peaceful location, rooms from FF300.

RESTAURANTS

Les Millésimes
Tel: 80 51 84 24
First-class cooking and amazing cellar
with some 45,000 bottles. Set menus
from FF300.

*Above and Right Two images of
Gevrey-Chambertin: a traditional
cellar and a chapel amongst vines.*

GEVREY-CHAMBERTIN

The village of Brochon lies just half a kilometre south of
Fixin, with its neighbouring village of Gevrey-Chambertin
a further 1.5 kilometres south along the D122 Route des
Grands Crus (13 kilometres south of Dijon).

It is thought that vines first started growing along the
hillside between these two villages during Roman times.
Certainly the Roman presence in this area has been con-
firmed by the excavation of sculptures from the period.

The vineyards on the slopes to the right of the road south
of Brochon are Premiers Crus, while a series of Grand Cru
vineyards extend to the right and left of the D122 directly
south of Gevrey-Chambertin.

The locals will tell you that the Clos de Bèze was the first
field in the region to be planted with grapevines in the 7th

century by the monks of the Abbey of Bèze. A farmer, called Bertin, later planted a plot of land next to it, *le champ de Bertin* and the wines from his vineyard enjoyed just as good a reputation as those of the Clos de Bèze, hence the vineyard came to be called Chambertin-Clos de Bèze. The village of Gevrey added the illustrious word Chambertin to its name by royal decree in 1847. No other village in Burgundy now has as many Grands Crus.

The other Grands Crus in the village are: Chapelle-Chambertin, Charmes-Chambertin (by far the largest), Griotte-Chambertin, Latricières-Chambertin, Mazis-Chambertin (also spelled Mazys and Mazi) and Ruchottes-Chambertin. In terms of quality, the three most interesting of these Grands Crus are Griotte, Latricières and Mazis.

In the village itself is the 10th-century castle with its angular towers and vaulted wine cellars, restored by the monks of Cluny. The church of Saint-Aignan is also interesting to visit with its beautiful wood carvings and decorated tombstones.

MOREY-SAINT-DENIS

The next village along the D122 is Morey-Saint-Denis. It is about three kilometres south of Gevrey-Chambertin and the road passes directly through the Grand Cru vineyards of Clos de Bèze, Chambertin and Latricières. The first vineyard to fall within the appellation boundary is the Grand Cru Clos de la Roche to the right of the road. The village's other famous Grand Cru vineyard, Clos de Tart, lies on the south side of the village. This vineyard is exclusively owned by Momessin and the cellars are worth a visit to see their excellently preserved 12th-century presses.

La Rôtisserie du Chambertin
Tel: 80 34 33 20
Refined cuisine. Menus from FF300.
La Sommellerie
Tel: 80 34 31 48
Regional dishes. Lunch with wine for FF100. Other menus from FF150.

RECOMMENDED PRODUCERS

Domaine Bachelet Great wines at all quality levels.
Philippe Batacchi/Domaine Clos Noir Sound, fragrant red wines.
Lucien Boillot et Fils Good wines include Nuits-St-Georges and Volnay.
Pierre Bourée Fils Small company making solid wines designed to last.
Alain Burguet Charming, balanced well-made wines.
Camus Père & Fils Brilliant range of sites. Implicit belief in *terroir*.
Domaine Pierre Damoy Owns largest single share of Clos de Bèze.
Domaine Drouhin-Laroze Distinguished estate. Pure, fairly light-coloured wines. Drink relatively early.
Philippe Leclerc Top estate. Wines have body, new oak and age well.
Domaine Maume Dark, lingering, intense, flawless wines.
Domaine Denis Mortet Balanced, firm wines, full of fruit.
Naigeon-Chauveau/Domaine des Varoilles Good value village wines. Also Domaine des Varoilles.
Joseph Roty Perfectionist wine-making. Refined and expressive wines.
Domaine Armand Rousseau Père & Fils Traditional classy wines with depth, elegance and individuality.

MOREY-ST-DENIS

HOTEL

Castel de Très Girard
Tel: 80 34 33 09
Good sized rooms with character from FF320. Menus from FF200.

RECOMMENDED PRODUCERS

Domaine Pierre Amiot et Fils Distinguished wines, firm, elegant, subtle and yet deeply flavoured.
Domaine Arlaud Père et Fils Classic red wines, top-quality.
Domaine Dujac Graceful – yet firm wines, elegant fruit and new oak.
Domaine des Lambrays Great improvement since new ownership in 1979. The result is a noble wine with vanilla aromas and intense fruit. In 1981 Grand Cru was granted.
Georges Lignier et Fils Fruity perfumed wines with a touch of oak, vanilla and firm tannin.

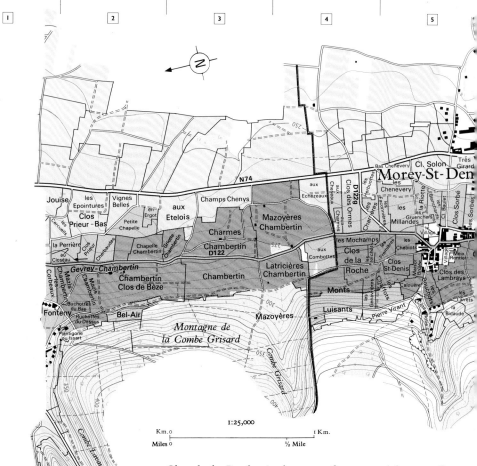

Clos de la Roche is the most famous and largest of Morey's five Grands Crus and gives powerful wines. Tasted blind they are much like the Grands Crus of Gevrey-Chambertin. Besides intensity, a good Clos de la Roche has elegance, fruit (wild cherries) and a hint of violets.

The Grand Cru to which Morey-Saint-Denis owes the second half of its name is Clos Saint-Denis. Clos des Lambrays extends between Clos de Tart and Clos Saint-Denis on the far side of the village from the road.

In the main, these wines hold the middle ground between the powerful wines of Gevrey-Chambertin to the north and the more elegant burgundies of Chambolle-Musigny to the south. Hugh Johnson has described them as the tenors, rather than sopranos or baritones in the Côte de Nuits choir.

CHAMBOLLE-MUSIGNY

For a little exercise, walk the kilometre along the D122 to the next wine village, Chambolle-Musigny. Nearing the village, you pass the famous Grand Cru vineyard of Bonnes Mares on the right, a tiny part of which actually lies within the Morey-Saint-Denis appellation.

Up to the late 1980s, the most interesting sites in Chambolle-Musigny were the late-Gothic village church with its striking tower and marvellous 16th-century frescos, and the ancient hollow lime tree in the churchyard. Then during the 1980s the Swiss wine estate, André Ziltener ren-

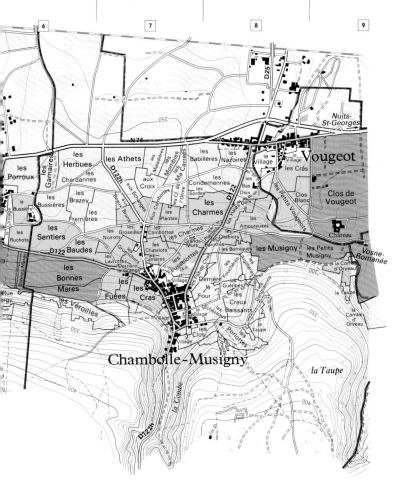

A

D25

Nuits-St-Georges

N74

les Herbues   les Athets   les Maladières   les Mombies   les Babillères   les Nazoires   le Village   le Village

Vougeot

B

les Porroux   les Gamaires   les Chardannes   aux Croix   aux Echanges   les Condemennes   les Crâs

la Bussière   les Bussières   les Brazey   les Combottes   les Cl. de Ma Carrée   les Sordes   les Plantes   Bas Doix   Clos Blanc   Clos de Vougeot

les Frémières   les Charmes

les Ruchots   les Sentiers   les Baudes   D122   les Groseilles   les Noirots   les Combottes   les Charmes   les Grands Murs   Plantes   les Chabiots   les Amoureuses   Château

D122   les Bonnes Mares   les Fuées   les Cras   les Véroilles   Derrière la Grange   les Chatelots   les Carrières   les Lavrottes   Gruenchers   les Fousselottes   les Barottes   les Borniques   **les Musigny**   les Petits Musigny   la Combe d'Orveau   **Vosne-Romanée**

C

Derrière le Village   le Village   les Guéripes   les Drazelles   la Taupe

les Fuées   le Four   les Creux   les Baissants   la Combe d'Orveau

le Village   l'Echezeau   le Village   les Portiottes   la Taupe

Chambolle-Musigny

les Clos   le Village   *la Taupe*

D

la Combe

D122h

E

Morey-Saint-Denis

········ ─ ···	Commune (parish) or Canton boundary	▢ Other vineyard
▬▬▬	Commune Appellation boundary	▢ Woods
▨	Grand Cru vineyard	═25═ Contour interval 5 metres
▨	Premier Cru vineyard	/ Internal vineyard boundary
▢	Commune Appellation vineyard	▨▨▨ Wine route

F

G

H

Left *Morey-St-Denis has clay and limestone soils and produces some of Burgundy's darkest, most long-living red wines and a rare white.*

I

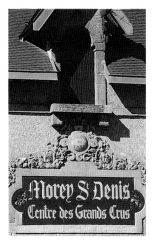

Above *Clos de Tart in Morey-St-Denis, a wine which has great depth of colour and flavour and considerable ageing potential.*

Domaine Hubert Lignier Fine wines at all levels.
Domaine Ponsot Concentrated reds: the Vieilles Vignes wines are the stars. Also white Morey-St-Denis.
Domaine B Serveau et Fils The Premiers Crus in particular develop into softly fruity, velvety wines.
Clos de Tart The renowned Grand Cru Clos de Tart smells of raspberries, strawberries and newly-felled oak.
J Taupenot-Merme Delicious wines. Charmes-Chambertin is best, but try the Morey-St-Denis.

CHAMBOLLE-MUSIGNY

HOTEL

Château André Ziltener
Tel: 80 62 81 37
Small, luxurious and expensive hotel.

RESTAURANT

Le Chambolle-Musigny
Tel: 80 62 86 26
Reasonably-priced restaurant serving local specialities and many local wines.

RECOMMENDED PRODUCERS

Domaine Bertheau Traditional producer; wines often keenly priced.
D Moine-Hudelot Characterful wines from well positioned vineyards.
Domaine J F Mugnier Musigny from Château de Chambolle-Musigny.
Domaine G Roumier Fantastic, unbeatable, aromatic burgundies.
Hervé Roumier Passionately made

ovated a local castle, renaming it Château André Ziltener. It is now a luxury hotel and the cellars have been made into a museum (open seven days a week).

The light, lime-bearing soil gives the red wines of Chambolle-Musigny the finest structure of the entire Côte de Nuits. They are full of subtlety, but structured enough to age excellently. The very best come from the Grand Cru Le Musigny. Bonnes Mares, the other Grand Cru, is softer, less delicate, but still delicious. Feminine grace and delicacy are just as strongly present in the wines of Premiers Crus such as the aptly named Amoureuses and Charmes.

VOUGEOT

At Chambolle-Musigny, the D122 Route des Grands Crus turns sharp left, leading down in a southeasterly direction. The village of Vougeot is just one kilometre along the road. At the T-junction, take the right turn for the village centre. On the other side of the village, instead of following the D122, which joins up with the N74, take the road forking off to the right, the Chemin du Clos de Vougeot. This takes you back up past the unmistakable, world-famous Clos de Vougeot vineyard on the left.

The village of Vougeot consists of little more than an 800-metre long street with several short side streets. Every year it attracts many thousands of visitors, and this is due to the fame of the Clos de Vougeot vineyard, whose history spans some 700 years.

Above *The patterned landscape of the vineyard Clos de Vougeot, with the striking château in the background.*

Left *The cellar of the Clos des Lambrays which was finally given Grand Cru status in 1981.*

Surrounded by a stone wall, the vineyard covers about 50 hectares and is divided between 70 owners, each on average owning less than one hectare. The Clos de Vougeot is actually a miniature Burgundy, because nowhere else is it so clear that the reputation and winemaking ability of a producer is more important than the name or status of a plot of land. It is generally agreed, though, that the top of the slope has better soil and produces higher-quality wines than the bottom, which can get waterlogged.

As you drive up the Chemin du Clos de Vougeot, you pass the Château de la Tour on the left, a scaled-down castle which was built in 1890. It belongs to the single largest owner of Clos de Vougeot land, the Domaine Château de la Tour. Situated almost at the top of the vineyard is the austere, 16th-century castle, Château de Vougeot, built by the monks of Cîteaux and, since 1944, the property of Les Chevaliers du Tastevin. This wine fraternity, founded in 1934 when the market for Burgundy wines was at a low ebb, has been incredibly successful in promoting the wines of Burgundy worldwide. The Confrérie holds enrolement ceremonies, banquets and tastings in the castle throughout the year but it is also a wine museum.

Next to the Clos de Vougeot, near the entrance to Château de Vougeot, is the Premier Cru Clos Blanc de Vougeot where a good, fruity white wine is made. The road follows the edge of the Clos de Vougeot vineyard, past the château and on towards Vosne-Romanée.

fruity red wines at all quality levels.
Domaine Comte Georges de Vogüé One of Burgundy's great names. The Musignys are the height of finesse. Small amount of white made.

VOUGEOT

HOTELS

Domaine Bertagna
Tel: 80 62 86 04
This wine estate has a dozen rooms. Prices starting at about FF300.
Château de Gilly (Gilly-lès-Cîteaux)
Tel: 80 62 89 98
Originally 14th-century Cistercian abbey. Prices start at FF700. Good food in cellar restaurant from FF200.

RECOMMENDED PRODUCERS

Domaine Bertagna Recent rise in quality. Also, rare white Vougeot.
Georges Clerget Well constructed, aromatic wines.
Michel Clerget Minimal production. Wonderful les Charmes.
Alain Hudelot-Noëllat Carefully vinified, formidable wines.
Bernard Munier (Gilly-lès-Cîteaux) Elegant red wines.
Château de la Tour Rich and fruity wine, occassionally lacking finesse.

VOSNE ROMANEE

RESTAURANTS

Losset
Tel: 80 62 88 10
By the church in Flagey-Echézeaux. Excellent, inexpensive regional food.
La Toute Petite Auberge
Tel: 80 61 02 03
Regional dishes. Menus from FF125.

VOSNE-ROMANEE

Continuing along towards Vosne-Romanée, be aware that you are approaching hallowed ground in terms of wine-making. On your left are the world-famous Grand Cru vineyards Les Grands Echézeaux and Echézeaux. These actually lie in the commune of Flagey-Echézeaux dividing Vougeot from Vosne-Romanée. At the T-junction, turn left down the hill and into the village of Vosne-Romanée.

No-one should visit Vosne-Romanée because of its architectural beauty, but the wine is another story. There are six Grands Crus within this municipality, some of them legendary around the world, and, although sometimes outrageously expensive, it is generally agreed that they represent Burgundy's finest wines, full of brilliant, concentrated, flavour, perfect balance and magical finesse.

The most famous is La Romanée-Conti, marked by gravelly red soil and a large stone cross. The present owner

Right Pruning – one of the most important vineyard tasks: here in the Romanée-Conti, with its distinguishing large stone cross.

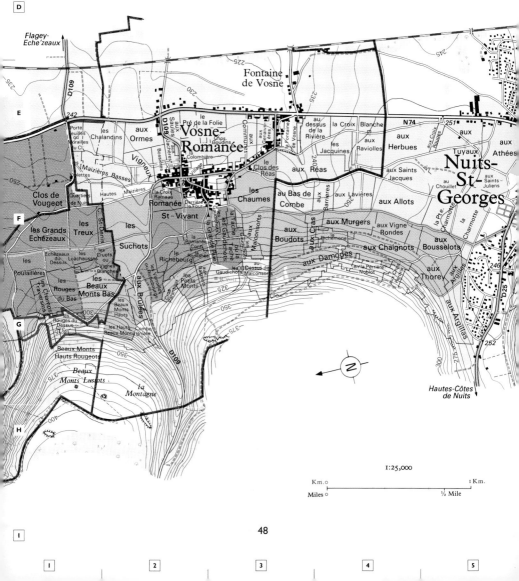

is the Domaine de la Romanée-Conti, established in 1942 and jointly owned by two families, Leroy and De Villaine.

The red wine La Romanée-Conti is exotically perfumed, richly nuanced, concentrated and complex with perfect balance. It needs at least ten years and then tastes both luxurious and satin-like. During the French Revolution, a document declared this to be the best wine, not only of the Côte d'Or vineyards, but of all the vineyards in France itself.

Another famous Grand Cru here is La Tâche, also owned entirely by the Domaine de la Romanée-Conti. This wine is somewhat earthier than that of La Romanée-Conti, and marvellously complex (spices, mushrooms, small red fruits, freshly mown grass). The other Grands Crus are: Le Richebourg (powerful, yet complex), La Romanée-Saint-Vivant (stylish, elegant), La Romanée (intense, deep-coloured), and La Grande Rue (firm, fine) which was promoted to Grand Cru status in 1991.

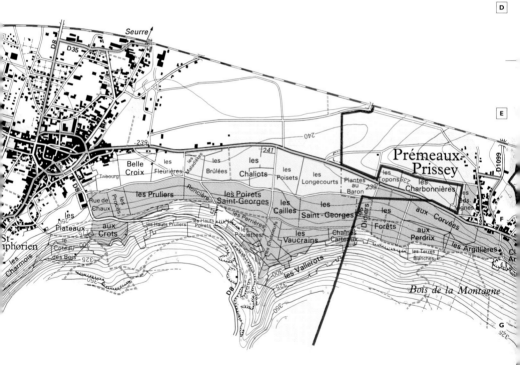

Nuits-Saint-Georges

Commune (parish) or Canton boundary	Other vineyard
Commune Appellation boundary	Woods
Grand Cru vineyard	Contour interval 5 metres
Premier Cru vineyard	Internal vineyard boundary
Commune Appellation vineyard	Wine route

RECOMMENDED PRODUCERS

Robert Arnoux Sometimes excellent, can be thin. Select carefully.
Jean Grivot Serious, high-quality wines. Recent Guy Accad supervision.
Domaine Jean Gros Top estate run by mother and son team.
Domaine Leroy Organic methods, tiny yields. Fine, ageworthy wines.
Domaine Méo-Camuzet Rich, elegant wines. Can be drunk young. Oak integrates well after a few years.
Mongeard-Mugneret Structured wines with velvety fruit.
Domaine G Mugneret-Gibourg Eight quality wines are made here, headed by a superb Clos de Vougeot.
Gérard et René Mugneret Reliable, unfiltered wines in wax-sealed bottles.
A Pernin-Rossin The Guy Accad touch again – deep purple colour, intense bramble aromas and rich fruit.
Domaine de la Romanée-Conti No wine estate is as famous as this – with prices to match. Average age of vines 45 years. New casks are used although some wine is unoaked. Several years' ageing always required.

NUITS-ST-GEORGES

HOTEL

La Gentilhommière
Tel: 80 61 12 06
On D25, west of Nuits. Rooms from FF400. Menus from FF180.

RESTAURANTS

Caveau Saint-Ugezon
Tel: 80 61 21 59
Inexpensive menus and reasonably priced wines. Good for lunch.
La Côte d'Or
Tel: 80 61 06 10
Refined cuisine. Special daily menu from FF150, ordinary menu starts at FF270. Large wine list. Also a hotel.

NUITS-SAINT-GEORGES

From the church in Vosne-Romanée, leave the village by taking the road towards the vineyard slopes. Turn left at the T-junction, left at the next and right at the following one. This takes you into Nuits-Saint-Georges.

The town is both the geographic and commercial centre of the Cote de Nuits. It is busy, not least because it is the location of *négociants*, liqueur-makers and fruit juice factories.

Nuits is modern but maintains a historic atmosphere. The main street, Rue Fagon, is named after the royal physician who cured Louis XIV with doses of the town's wine.

The heart of Nuits is the Place de la République. It has a 17th-century clock tower (*beffroi*) housing an archeological museum. On the west side of the town is the beautiful Saint-Symphorien church. On the south side, the Hospice Saint-Laurent has a remarkable statue of the Virgin Mary.

Just as in Beaune, vineyards have been donated to the hospitals of Nuits and wines are auctioned shortly before Easter. They are mainly Premiers Crus from Nuits-Saint-Georges and their average quality is high. Wines from the

north side of the town, nearest to Vosne, have a silky rich-
ness reminiscent of Vosne wines. Those from the south of
Nuits, closer to Prémeaux, tend to be rougher and more
vegetal, and need cellaring.

The best-known Premiers Crus are Les Saint-Georges,
Les Vaucrains, Les Pruliers and Les Porrets. Typical Nuits-
Saint-Georges has a muscular flavour and firm tannin. Lighter
types are also made which are good when young, with supple fruitiness. Some white grapes are harvested, from which,
amongst others, a luxuriant white, La Perrière, is made.

For a unique tasting, visit Le Berchère which is owned
by Moillard and situated on the northern side of the town.
Visitors can taste up to 20 wines, arranged by themes.

Nuits-Saint-Georges is also the base for the controversial
consultant winemaker, Guy Accad, who has dozens of illustrious clients in the Côte d'Or. His aim is to make deeply-
coloured, aromatic wines that age. His methods include
careful soil analysis, restricted yields, super-ripe grapes and a
cold, extended skin maceration before a long, cool fermentation. To date, the results are successful – powerful wines
that are ageing as desired and in much demand.

The appellation Nuits-Saint-Georges also extends to the
southern neighbouring municipality Prémeaux.

Le Sanglier
Tel: 80 61 04 79
Rural inn on D25. Inexpensive menus
with grilled meat dishes a speciality.

RECOMMENDED PRODUCERS

Marcel Bocquenet Conscientious
winemaking, attractive wines.
Jean Claude Boisset One of the
most influential négociants in Côte
d'Or. Owns, among others, Lionel J
Bruck, Jaffelin, Pierre Ponnelle,
Ropiteau Frères and Charles Viénot.
Jean Chauvenet Strong stylish reds.
Robert Chevillon Reliable quality.
Joseph Faiveley Among the leaders
in Burgundy. Well structured, soundly
balanced and generous reds; the
whites are fresh and of similar quality.
Domaine Henri Gouges Recently
vast improvements have been seen;
white La Perrière is rare and fragrant.
Labouré-Roi One of Burgundy's
largest négociants-éleveurs. Excellent
wines reflecting their commune styles.
Alain Michelot A top estate.
Aromatic wines with an elegant
firmness and great purity.
Moillard Has its own vineyards and
is also a négociant-éleveur. Wines can
be excellent – supple and generous.

PLACE OF INTEREST

From Nuits it is only 11 kilometres to
the abbey of Cîteaux (heading east).
There, monks make delicious cheese.

Far left *Methusalems of Romanée-
Conti in cellar of the domaine.*
Mid left *The vines of Grands
Echezeaux.*
Left *Tools for training vines.*
Above *Grape pickers setting off to
harvest at Romanée-Conti.*

PREMEAUX-PRISSY

🍽 RESTAURANTS

Auberge de la Miotte
Ladoix-Serrigny
Tel: 80 26 40 75
18th-century former hunting lodge behind the church in Serrigny. Coq au vin, boeuf bourguignon, cuisse de canard au baies de cassis and other regional dishes are served at very reasonable prices. Menus start at about FF75.

Les Coquines
Ladoix-Serrigny (Buisson)
Tel: 80 26 43 58
Situated on the route nationale, this restaurant serves great food. The cooking is inventive and attention has been paid to the interior. Menus starting at around FF140.

🍇 RECOMMENDED PRODUCERS

Domaine Bertrand Ambroise
This small estate produces delicious wines.

Domaine de l'Arlot
Established at the end of the 19th century by Jules Belin. Bought by AXA Millésimes in the second half of the 1980s, it has risen again in full glory with its Nuits-St-Georges Premier Cru Clos de l'Arlot, white and red. Try also the Clos des Forêts, and St-Georges Premiers Crus and the Côte de Nuits-Villages.

Robert Dubois & Fils
Dynamic, highly skilled, progressive wine-growing family producing richly coloured, powerful, aromatic wines of a good standar , such as the Côte de Nuits-Villages, Nuits-St-Georges

Above *Harvesting in Burgundy can be frenetic and exhausting work.*
Left *Vine pruning must be carried out with extreme care to ensure quality grapes for years to come.*

Right *A vine-covered outbuilding at Clos de l'Arlot, one of the most important properties of Nuits-St-Georges.*
Far right *Nuits-St-Georges with its vines in foreground.*

PREMEAUX-PRISSEY

To get from Nuits–Saint-Georges to Aloxe-Corton, you cannot avoid using a stretch of the N74. Only the first section of the route (about ten kilometres), between Nuits and Prémeaux-Prissey, is surrounded by vineyards. It is worth taking a quick detour at Prémeaux by turning left in order to view the small, pretty church with its multicoloured roof.

By driving downhill and keeping to the right, you pass the Château de Prémeaux, where there is a small wine estate. The village of Prémeaux-Prissey runs seamlessly into Comblanchien which, in turn, borders the village of Corgoloin. These three villages come within the Côtes de Nuits–Villages appellation. In the best vineyard in Corgoloin, the walled Clos des Langres, there is a sign which marks the boundary between the Côte de Beaune and the Côte de Nuits. In the marvellous cellars of the Clos des Langres, built by Cistercian monks, is a magnificent wine press from the 18th century.

and Nuits-St-Georges Les Poirets St-Georges.

Domaine Jean-Jacques Confuron
Quite a large estate with a fine range of vineyards, managed by Sophie and Alain Meunier. Delightful wines from Nuits-St-Georges and Chambolle-Musigny, plus Clos de Vougeot and Romanée-St-Vivant.

Domaine Daniel Rion & Fils
Modern equipped estate located along the *route nationale*. Clear tasting wines, with hints of oak, and aromas of red berry fruits. Nuits-St-Georges and Vosne-Romanée are excellently represented by several fine Premiers Crus.

PLACES OF INTEREST

After having been closed for years, the Clos des Langres in Corgoloin is now open to visitors. The estate is run by La Reine Pédauque from Aloxe-Corton and produces a good Côte de Nuits-Villages.

LADOIX-SERRIGNY

RECOMMENDED PRODUCERS

Capitain-Gagnerot
Reliable wines, with Corton-Charlemagne and Corton Les Renardes as its stars. The Ladoix La Micaude is also worth discovering.

Chevalier Père & Fils
Extremely hospitable winegrowing family (they live in Buisson) who produce fine white wines in particular, including Ladoix and Corton-Charlemagne. The most appealing of the reds are those from the commune of Ladoix itself.

Prince Florent de Mérode
The Prince is of Belgian origin and his family have owned this property since 1700. He lives in a moated castle opposite his Corton vineyards. The wines from this estate are all strong Cortons of a high quality.

Domaine André Nudant & Fils
Rather large property with good portfolio of white and red wines.

Both Comblanchien and Corgoloin are dominated by stone quarries rather than vineyards. The beige marble-like stone of Comblanchien was used, among other things, for the Opéra in Paris and Orly airport.

LADOIX

Staying on the N74, you arrive after a few more kilometres, at the village of Ladoix (Ladoix-Serrigny) which has an attractive, small castle (which cannot be visited) and, near the exit to Aloxe-Corton, the chapel of Notre-Dame de la Chemin (11th- and 15th-century). Wines made here can be labelled under the appellations of Ladoix, Côte de Beaune-Villages; the better sited vineyards are sold generally as Aloxe-Corton Premier Cru. As the appellation of Ladoix itself is still relatively unknown, this village is a great source of excellent quality, good value Pinot Noir. A small amount of white wine is also produced, made either from Chardonnay or Pinot Blanc.

The Côte de Nuits

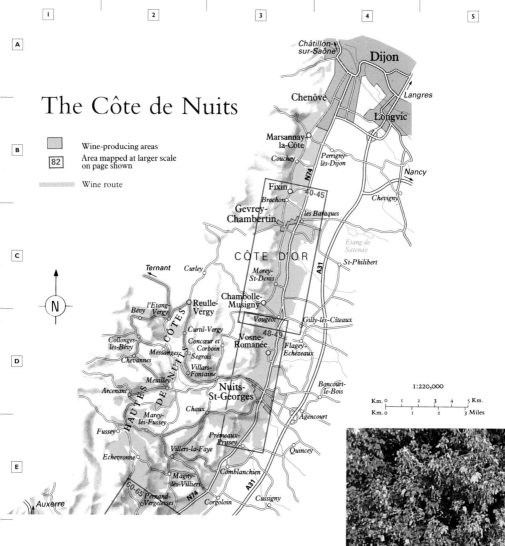

Wine-producing areas

82 Area mapped at larger scale on page shown

Wine route

HAUTES-COTES DE NUITS

If you take the D25 road west from the northern outskirts of the village of Nuits-Saint-Georges, you will find yourself travelling up the vineyard-covered slopes into the Hautes-Côtes de Nuits.

Vines have been recorded on the Hautes-Côtes de Nuits from as early as AD761. The area was granted the right to its own appellation conrôlée in 1961 and vineyard plantings proceeded initially mainly with Pinot Noir. But, as this area is on ground an average of 100 metres higher than either the Côte de Beaune or the Côte de Nuits, the air is colder and moves quickly through the little valleys between the hills. This presents conditions not quite so suitable for vines, and that is why only the slopes facing between southeast and southwest are planted with vineyards. It is not easy to ripen Pinot Noir successfully here, Chardonnay is much easier to cultivate. That is probably why the red burgundies from this region generally have less depth than those from the Côte de Nuits – but its also worth bearing in mind that they are less expensive. The white wines (including Bourgogne Aligoté)

are usually better than the reds in terms of quality, even though – as the predominating red grape vines indicate – more red wines are usually produced. Many growers also make Cassis or Framboise.

From the point of view of a tourist, Hautes-Côtes de Nuits is just as interesting as Côte de Nuits. Indeed, the landscape is, in many ways, far prettier up on these higher slopes. A few of the most picturesque villages are situated along the route picked out here.

Left *Many crops are grown in the Hautes-Côtes de Nuits, carrots and asparagus, as well as grapes.*
Below *A beautiful autumnal scene. Following this, when winter arrives, all the spring and summer's growth is removed and only a couple of short canes will remain of the vine.*

HAUTES COTES DE NUITS

HOTEL

Hôtel le Manassès
Tel: 80 61 43 81 (Curtil-Vergy)
Peaceful hotel, opened in 1991, has seven neat rooms combining modern comfort with rustic ambiance. Guests are offered a complementary wine-tasting session.

RESTAURANTS

Auberge la Ruelée
Tel: 80 61 44 11 (Curtil-Vergy)
Rural inn, in walking distance from the local hotel. Inexpensive menus from about FF100. Regional cuisine. There is a small terrace at the rear.

By taking the D25 road from (the direction of) Nuits-Saint-Georges and then taking the D35 after the restaurant Le Sanglier, you pass the steep vineyard Les Genièvres and the tiny hamlet of Villars-Fontaine with its modest little castle. A beautiful road then leads up to the village of Curtil-Vergy – travelling this route you will pass the ruins of an early monastery.

Drive on northwards and you will come to Reulle-Vergy which has a regional museum to look at, an old bathing place and the church of Saint-Saturnin which has fine views looking down on to the village. Then follow the winding road to the next settlement, Ternant. When you go past this village, in the direction of Rolle, two dolmen can be seen in the middle of the forest (and close to the road). Rolle also has a nice restaurant.

Go back to l'Etang-Vergy by way of the village of Ternant again. The overgrown walls of the former castle can be seen by driving towards Bévy and then looking back along the direction you came. Bévy itself is distinguished by its church tower, which has an unusual copper dome.

A beautiful road runs from Bévy to Collonges-lès-Bévy, with its 17th-century castle. After this comes Chevannes, which has a small, old church with a classic Burgundian multicoloured spire. Then proceed to Arcenant via Meuilly. Apart from wine, fruit liqueurs are produced here.

Continue south to Marey-lès-Fussey with its Romanesque church and the Maison des Hautes-Côtes restaurant, notable for its beautiful views. From Marey, you can either return to Nuits-Saint-Georges, or continue to Comblanchien or Corgoloin by way of Villars-la-Faye on the D115.

Ferme de Rolle
Hameau de Rolle (near Ternant)
Tel: 80 61 40 10
Cosy restaurant situated in an old farm. Regional cuisine. The façade is decorated with a red apple.
Maison des Hautes-Côtes
Tel: 80 62 91 29 (Marey-lès-Fussey)
Regional wines, with strictly traditional

Burgundian dishes. Three menus, each costing less than FF100. Various producers display their wines here.

RECOMMENDED PRODUCERS

Yves Chaley/Domaine du Val de Vergy (Curtil-Vergy) Modern technology here results in pure, delicious wines. There is also a hotel.
Domaine Marcel et Bernard Fribourg (Villers-la-Faye) Fruity white and good-quality red wines. Try the Bourgogne Aligoté and both red and white Hautes-Côtes de Nuits.
Domaine Bernard Hudelot-Verdel (Villars-Fontaine) One of the pioneers of Hautes-Côtes. Charming white Hautes-Côtes de Nuits and an oaky red wine.
Jayer-Gilles (Magny-lès-Villers) Excellent red wines are made here. Most of them – Echézeaux, Côte de Nuits-Villages, red Bourgogne, Hautes-Côtes de Nuits – are distinctly oaky.
Henri Naudin-Ferran (Magny-lès-Villers) Fine white Hautes-Côtes de Nuits made with half Chardonnay and half Pinot Blanc and subtle use of new oak. Bourgogne Aligoté and red Côte de Nuits-Villages are also good.
Domaine Thévenot-Le-Brun & Fils (Marey-lès-Fussey) Large properties making an unusually high proportion of white wine, including a Bourgogne Aligoté *perlant*.
Alain Verdet (Arcenant) Fine organically produced wines, fruity, lively and complex – with a guarantee from the winemaker that 'If you have a headache from my wines I will give you your money back'.

Left *Rose bushes planted at the end of rows of vines are more frequently seen in the Médoc than here in Burgundy.*

Above *The Côte d'Or has many picturesque features to captivate the visitor, such as here in the village of Savigny-lès-Beaune.*

The Côte de Beaune

The Côte de Beaune begins seamlessly just south of Prémeaux. If you can spot any noticable difference, it will be merely a variation in the colour of the soil. The Côte de Beaune generally has less iron in the soil and more chalk, and hence is less red in colour. This explains the lighter style of red wine produced and the extraordinary suitability of Chardonnay which thrives in such conditions.

ALOXE-CORTON

From Ladoix take the N74 for one kilometre and then turn right into Aloxe-Corton. As you leave Ladoix, the flat-topped hill of Corton is on your right. The wooded summit rises to almost 390 metres and its south and east facing slopes have more than 200 hectares of vines, nearly all Grands Crus.

History has it that King Charlemagne was crazy about the red wines of Aloxe, but often spilled them on his white beard. His mother, Berthe au Grand Pied (the queen, with one foot larger than the other), complained so much that he commanded the vineyard be replanted with white grapes. A great wine was not the result: Aligoté was planted and only in the last century did Chardonnay replace it.

With this a great white wine was born: extremely full with a rich aroma with ripe fruit, oak, honey and cinnamon. In honour of Charlemagne it was called Corton-Charlemagne. Its vineyard, a Grand Cru, is on the southeast slope of the Corton hill. The other slopes give red Corton, similarly formidable; firm wines with style and distinction.

Aloxe-Corton has a fine 15th-century castle, Château Corton-André, owned by the *négociant* house La Reine Pédauque. It has a multicoloured roof and is open to visitors, although the winery is modern, large and lacklustre. The delightful Hotel Clarion is nearby. On the village square there is a *caveau*, where wines can be tasted and bought.

Left A view of Pernand Vergelesses which produces both red and white wines, the whites being a little more appoachable when young.

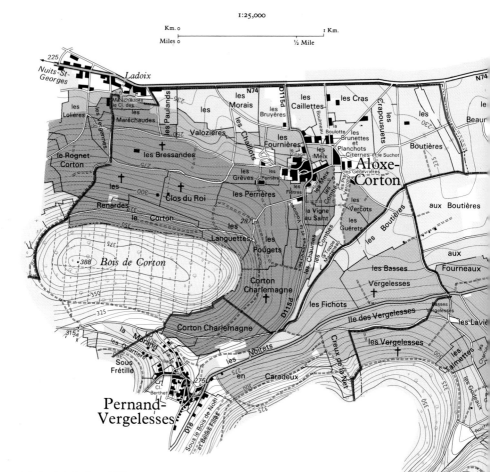

Km. 0   1:25,000   1 Km.
Miles 0   ½ Mile

PERNAND-VERGELESSES

Instead of racing straight on to Pernand-Vergelesses, it is certainly worth taking time to drive up the Corton hill. You get a beautiful view of Aloxe-Corton and its surroundings this way. To do this, leave the village on the D115d to Pernand-Vergelesses and take the first exit to the right.

To reach Pernand-Vergelesses, you rejoin the D115d and continue northwest, skirting the southwest slopes of the Corton hill. The village is to its west, hidden in a valley.

The name Pernand is derived from the French for 'lost spring', and Vergelesses refers to the Premier Cru vineyard, Les Vergelesses. The chapel of Notre-Dame de Bonne Espérance stands on a hill and was built here in 1854 in gratitude for the reconversion to Catholicism of a prominent local woman. There is an excellent view from here.

Pernand-Vergelesses' most famous inhabitant was Jacques Copeau. He made a name for himself in Paris as a theatrical innovator, then settled in Pernand where, with young actors, he formed a new theatre group. It was called Les Copiaux, based on an idea of the local postman. Their performances were announced by trumpet flourishes, taking place in village squares or parks. Copeau (1879–1949) is buried in Pernand.

Below *One of Burgundy's most distinctive landmarks is the roof of coloured tiles – these belong to the Château of Aloxe-Corton.*

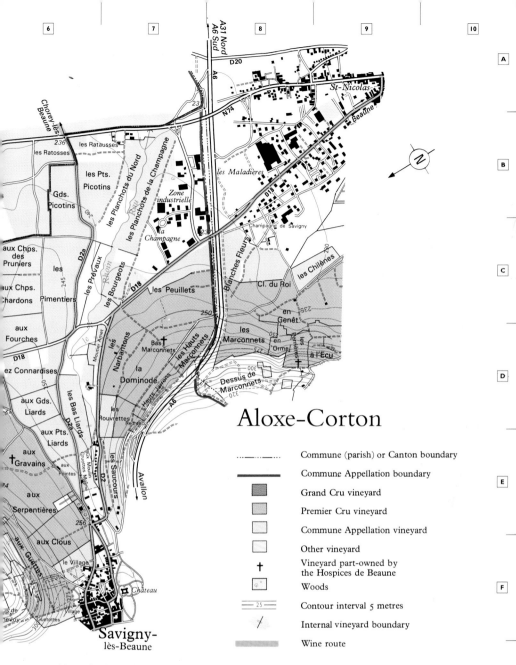

Aloxe-Corton

Commune (parish) or Canton boundary
Commune Appellation boundary
Grand Cru vineyard
Premier Cru vineyard
Commune Appellation vineyard
Other vineyard
† Vineyard part-owned by the Hospices de Beaune
Woods
Contour interval 5 metres
Internal vineyard boundary
Wine route

Although the village produces considerably more red than white wine, the white is generally more attractive. Red Pernand-Vergelesses in its youth tends to taste rather tight and therefore benefits from a few years' bottle age.

SAVIGNY-LES-BEAUNE

Leave Pernand-Vergelesses by retracing the route back to Aloxe-Corton on the D18. Instead of taking the left fork onto the D115d back down to Aloxe, keep straight on. After about two kilometres turn right towards Savigny-lès-Beaune. This is a spectacular drive, with some fine views.

The history of Savigny goes back to the Gallic-Romanic period, but nowadays the village acts as a modern commuter suburb of Beaune. The old centre still retains its historic

Below Paniers *of grapes stacked up at harvesting time.*
Right and below right *Around Beaune there are many imposing buildings. These châteaux are in Aloxe-Corton and Savigny.*

ALOXE-CORTON

HOTEL

Hôtel Clarion
Tel: 80 26 46 70
Owned by Voarick. From FF500.

RECOMMENDED PRODUCERS

Maurice Chapuis Luxurious wines with depth and power.
Caves de la Reine Pédauque Large firm. Best wines from own sites and include Corton-Charlemagne.
Domaine Daniel Senard Excellent wines. Fine rare white Aloxe-Corton.
Michel Voarick Traditional, long-living wines of real class and quality.

PERNAND-VERGELESSES

RESTAURANT

Le Charlemagne
Tel: 80 21 51 45
Great value regional dishes.

RECOMMENDED PRODUCERS

Domaine Bonneau du Martray Thought to be the site of Emperor Charlemagne's vineyards. Now one of the largest and best reputed local properties.
Domaine Dubrueil-Fontaine Bernard Dubrueil makes delicate red Ile des Vergelesses and powerful Cortons.

atmosphere, which you can sample in a visit to the church, with its 12th-century clock tower and octagonal spire. Inside is a 15th-century fresco depicting angels and saints.

It is only a few minutes' walk from the church to the castle, in the middle of a park on the south side of the village. The imposing building, flanked by round towers, is now a museum housing a collection of a few hundred motorcycles, racing cars and aeroplanes (including a Mirage III). Visitors enter by way of an annex, the so-called Petit Château, which dates from 1683 and was built in the form of an arch.

Wander through the village, particularly down the *rues* Chanoine Donin and Guy de Vaulchier, searching out the 15 or more wall inscriptions. They date from between the 17th and 19th centuries, and act as 'thoughts for the day', such as: *Il ne faut pas donner son appât au goujon quand on peut esperer prendre une carpe* (never give the bait to a gudgeon, when there's a chance you could catch a carp); and *Malgré les impostuers, traîtres et jaloux, l'homme patient viendra à bout de tout* (despite impostors, scoundrels and the jealous, he who waits comes out on top). No-one knows who wrote these or why.

If you drive towards Beaune from the castle, you will see in a side street to the right the Manoir de Nicolay, a large Louis XIV-style mansion. Behind it is a marvellous garden. This is all part of the Chandon de Briailles wine estate.

Domaine Laleure-Piot
High-quality, fruity wines. Reds are best.
Domaine Pavelot
Good whites and reds from the village.
Domaine Rapet Père & Fils
Well known for white Sous la Vierge,
Corton-Charlemagne and red 1er Cru.

SAVIGNY-LES-BEAUNE

HOTELS

Lud'Hôtel
Tel: 80 21 53 24
Peaceful hotel with rooms (from
FF300). Restaurant and swimming pool.
l'Ouvrée
Tel: 80 21 51 52
Comfortable rooms from FF260.
Sound menu: four courses for FF100.

RESTAURANT

La Cuverie
Tel: 80 21 50 03
Simple, rustic regional restaurant.

RECOMMENDED PRODUCERS

Simon Bize & Fils
Stylish, tasty wines and always a
smiling welcome.
Bonnot-Lamblot
Traditional methods. Good wines.
Capron-Manieux
Tiny quantities, but always high quality
including both red and white Savignys.
Domaine de Chandon de Briailles
Flawless Savigny, Pernand-Vergelesses
and Aloxe-Corton wines.
Maison Doudet-Naudin
An old-fashioned *négociant* firm now
now making rich, supple fruity reds.
Domaine Antonin Guyon
Pure, lively-tasting wines with an
attractive wood/vanilla aroma.

CHOREY-LES-BEAUNE

HOTEL

Château de Chorey
Tel: 80 22 06 05
The castle has six large, comfortable
rooms. Prices start at about FF600.

RESTAURANT

L'Ermitage-Corton
Tel: 80 22 05 28
Excellent cooking. Large wine list.
Menus from FF300. Also hotel.

RECOMMENDED PRODUCERS

Château de Chorey
Wines of great style and firm tannin.
Tollot-Beaut & Fils
Good, balanced reds and whites.

CHOREY-LES-BEAUNE

Chorey-lès-Beaune is on almost flat land. Although there
are no Grands Crus here, the lack of slopes is not necessarily
a handicap for making good wine, as proven by local estates.
The best have a rather sturdy structure and a soft fruitiness.

Château de Chorey is of most interest here. The main
building is 17th-century, the towers flanking it 13th. Around
it are a moat and park. Wine has been made here for centuries, and on the beams in the *cuverie* are etched a few striking harvest dates: in 1893 it began as early as August 28th.

BEAUNE

Leave Savigny-lès-Beaune from the south side of the village travelling in a westerly direction. At the four-way junction, turn right onto the D2 towards Beaune, with the slopes of the Montagne de Beaune on your right. The D2 joins the D18 which leads you straight into the town, crossing over the A6 on the way.

Beaune is the wine capital of Burgundy. Commercially, it is ideally placed near the junction of the A6 and the A31, but the attractiveness of the city itself undoubtedly plays a role, the ancient buildings giving Beaune huge historical importance.

The old centre is fantastically preserved and unusually rich in atmosphere. Beaune was probably founded in 52AD by Julius Caesar. The Dukes of Burgundy lived here at the beginning of the 13th century before they moved to Dijon and their palace still stands today. In fact, because so many of the town's medieval buildings have been used for storing wine, they have been carefully preserved. Many of the former

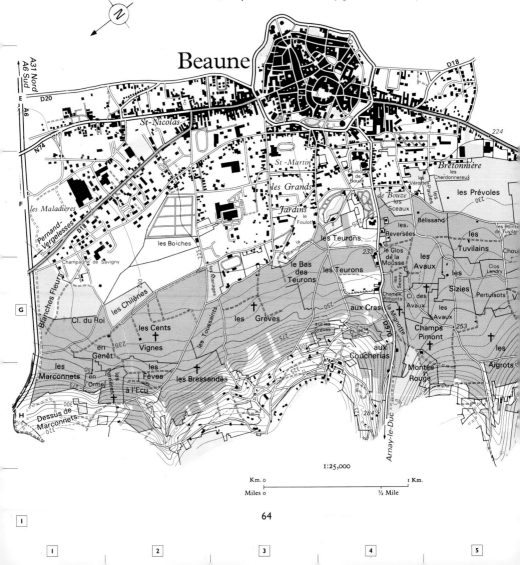

1:25,000

Above *An example of the rich variety of architecture to be discovered in Burgundy, the beautifully decorative Hôtel Dieu is not only one of the most famous, but one of the most stunning of sights.*

Beaune

....	Commune (parish) or Canton boundary
▬▬▬	Commune Appellation boundary
▨	Premier Cru vineyard
☐	Commune Appellation vineyard
☐	Other vineyard
✝	Vineyard part-owned by the Hospices de Beaune
☐	Woods
═ 25 ═	Contour interval 5 metres
/	Internal vineyard boundary
▦	Wine route

Beaune is full of wonderful places to stock up on food and wine. There are cheese shops such as this (right) and numerous wine shops (below).

BEAUNE

 HOTELS

Hostellerie de Bretonnière
43 Faubourg Bretonnière
Tel: 80 22 15 77
Convenient and close to the centre.
Private car park. Ask for a room at the
rear. Good rooms are about FF400.

Central Hôtel
2 Rue Victor-Millot
Tel: 80 24 77 24
Close to the Hôtel-Dieu. Nice rooms
and menus (starting at about FF400
and FF170). Very good regional cuisine.

Le Cep
27 Rue Maufoux
Tel: 80 22 35 48
Luxurious, stylish rooms (starting at
FF550). Traditionally prepared dishes
are served – the least expensive
(about FF170 on weekdays) are
recommended.

La Closerie
61 Route de Pommard
Tel: 80 22 15 07
Modern hotel with good rooms, a
garden and a swimming pool. Prices
starting at around FF350.

Colvert Golf Hôtel
Levernois
Tel: 80 24 78 20
Modern hotel with 24 comfortable
rooms (FF320 to FF350), next to
Beaune's golf course (other side of
the *autoroute*). Peace is assured.

Le Parc
Levernois
Tel: 80 24 63 00
Rather rustic rooms (starting at about
FF200). Peacefully situated, next to
the Hostellerie de Levernois.

RESTAURANTS

Au Bon Accueil
La Montagne
Tel: 80 22 08 80
On a hill near Beaune. Simple and
inexpensive restaurant which is very
popular. Regional cuisine.

Le Bénaton
25 Faubourg Bretonnière
Tel: 80 22 00 26
Simply furnished, but with inventive
dishes. Menus start at about FF150.
Less expensive weekday lunch menu.

moats are now gardens and it is possible to walk round the ancient battlements.

The best and most pleasant way of getting to know Beaune is to take a walk through the town. Begin in the central square, Place Carnot, where you can park. On the corner of Rue Carnot and the square is an excellent wine shop, Denis Perret. Leave the square, walking north along Rue Carnot, until you come to Place Monge, dominated by its 14th-century belfry with a remarkable wooden roof.

Now turn right into Rue des Tonneliers which is lined with dignified 18th-century houses. At the end of the street turn left and then immediately right into Rue Rousseau-Deslandes. Number ten along here is one of the most remarkable buildings in Beaune – the Hôtel de Cîteaux, which was built at the end of the 12th century. Continue by turning right into the Rue de Lorraine. On the corner stands the Hospice de la Charité with its chapel and courtyard.

Follow the Rue de Lorraine and then turn right along a small side street to the Hôtel de Ville, a 17th-century former Ursuline convent which now also houses two museums, the Musée des Beaux-Arts and the Musée Marey which is devoted to Etienne-Jules Marey, who developed the earliest principles of photographic technique.

Now turn back towards Rue de Lorraine. At the end of the street on your right you will see the most beautiful of Beaune's town gates, the Porte Saint-Nicolas. Near this gate are the Chapelle de l'Oratoire, where art exhibitions are sometimes held, and the cellars of the firm La Reine Pédauque which you can visit.

Continue the walk by turning left and following part of the old town walls. The round Bastion des Filles (or de l'Oratoire) on the corner of Boulevard Foch now serves as an above-ground wine cellar for Chanson Père & Fils. Now turn left back into the old town on Rue Paul Chanson, also called Rue du Collège. On the right is the entrance to Patriarche Père & Fils, whose cellars really do deserve a visit. You pay a small charge, which goes to charity, and you can taste an extensive range of wines.

Now turn right, walking south along Rue Gandelot to the basilica of Notre-Dame. Despite much alteration and rebuilding, this church still has clear traces of Burgundian Romanesque architecture. From April to November marvellous wall tapestries depicting the 'Life of the Virgin' are displayed.

It is only a minute's walk from here to the Musée du Vin de Bourgogne, one of France's most exciting museums, tucked away to the south of Notre-Dame. The museum, the 15th- and 16th-century former residence of the Dukes of Burgundy, houses a rich collection of objects and works of art connected with wine.

Taking the Rue d'Enfer (with the offices of the firm Joseph Drouhin at number seven) you come to the Avenue de la République. Turn left and then take the first street on the right which will bring you to a square with shops, including some selling wine. Also on this square is the hall where the Hospices de Beaune auction is held, the Office du Tourisme and, the climax of this walk, the Hôtel-Dieu.

Built in 1451, the Hôtel-Dieu was commissioned by Nicolas de Rolin, chancellor under Philip the Good. He

Le Bistro Bourguignon
8 Rue Monge
Tel: 80 22 23 24
Wine bar often offering burgundies by the glass. Inexpensive daily menu.

Chez Joël D
45 Rue Maufoux
Tel: 80 24 71 28
Specialities: oysters, seafood.

La Ciboulette
69 Rue Lorraine
Tel: 80 24 70 72
Pleasant place for good food, from fresh ingredients, for FF100 or less.

l'Ecusson
Place Malmédy
Tel: 80 24 03 82
Chic restaurant. One of Beaune's best. Original dishes – from about FF135.

Le Gourmandin
8 Place Carnot
Tel: 80 24 07 88
Inexpensive, regional dishes. burgundies available by the glass or *pichet*.

Le Grand Blue
Place au Beurre
Tel: 80 24 70 70
Freshwater and saltwater fish in very affordable à la carte menus.

Le Jardin des Remparts
10 Rue de l'Hôtel-Dieu
Tel: 80 24 79 41
Refined, contemporary dishes. The weekday lunch menu is about FF140. Ordinary menus start at about FF180.

Hostellerie de Levernois
Levernois
Tel: 80 24 73 58
Jean Crotet (formerly of La Côte d'Or in Nuits) has built a luxurious hotel complex, ten minutes' from Beaune. The cuisine is of a high quality and uses fresh regional ingredients. Weekday lunch costs about FF200, ordinary menus about FF400.

Hostellerie de la Paix
47 Faubourg Madeleine
Tel: 80 22 33 33
Two restaurants, the Rôtisserie (menus at about FF120) and Le Bouchon (FF100 or less), also a small hotel.
Relais de Saulx
6 Rue Louis-Véry
Tel: 80 22 01 35
Small, stylish, busy restaurant with reliable, rather conservative cuisine. Menus start at about FF125.

RECOMMENDED PRODUCERS

Domaine Besançenot-Mathouillet Medium-sized family estate owning vineyards mainly in Beaune itself. Some of the best Premiers Crus are Cent Vignes, Clos du Roi and Theurons.
Albert Bichot Modern, dynamic, successful exporters. Most wines are reliable, but some are excellent, eg Long-Depaquit in Chablis and Clos Frantin in Vosne-Romanée.
Bouchard Père & Fils Wines from own Grands and Premiers Crus vineyards. Bouchard is distributor for a number of other producers. After a major fire in 1989, they re-equipped with the latest technology. All wines are of above average quality.
J Calvet & Cie Chiefly middle-ranking wines. Guided tours are taken through its 15th-century wine cellars.
Domaine Cauvard Père & Fils Quality-conscious estate: good red and white Bourgognes Les Monts Battois.

Above *The delights to discover in a Beaune charcuterie.*
Above right *The intricately patterned roof of the Hôtel Dieu.*

and his wife, Guigone de Salins, decided to build a home for the sick and poor. The building was in use as an old people's home until as recently as 1971. Now it is mainly used as a museum. It must have been quite an experience for the patients, because their accommodation had the air of a palace rather than that of a hospital. The sickroom borders on a magnificent paved courtyard from where you look up to see a wooden veranda and gallery, and a superb multicoloured roof of glazed roof-tiles. There is a hall for the sick with 28 places for beds, an enormous kitchen, a dispensary and a second courtyard with statues of Nicolas Rolin and his wife. There is also an exhibition of tapestries and furniture as well as the magnificent alterpiece by Rogier van der Weyden, The Last Judgement (1443), which was specially commissioned by the Hospices de Beaune and is one of the transcendental masterpieces of Flemish art. This building alone justifies a visit to Beaune.

In the course of the centuries, various benefactors have left no less than 60 hectares of wine land to the Hôtel-Dieu. The wines from this land are sold at an annual auction to benefit the collective hospitals of Beaune, the Hospices de Beaune. This takes place on the third Sunday of November, and is the world's largest charity auction. The selling of wines is the highlight of Les Trois Glorieuses, the three days of celebration throughout the whole of Burgundy, at which time, in Beaune and other wine villages, there are tasting sessions and receptions.

From the Hôtel-Dieu it is only a minute's walk back to the Place Carnot.

Wine can be bought everywhere in Beaune with wine stores on every street. Beaune is also one of the largest wine communes of the Côte d'Or. The majority of the wine produced here is red. They seldom have striking individual characteristics, but are supple when young and can be left to mature for ten years or more. Centuries ago, Erasmus sighed that he wished to live in France, 'not to lead armies, but to drink the wines of Beaune'.

It is also possible to look at Beaune from above. Two different companies organize trips by hot air ballon over the vineyards and villages of the Côte. A firm called Beaune Autrement offers guided walks round the town's ramparts and courtyards as well as a tour of first growth vineyards and a visit to the American Camp where, in 1918, thousands of American soldiers camped on their way home from the war. Details of all these can be found in the Office du Tourisme.

Champy Père & Cie The oldest *négociant-éleveur* in Burgundy, with price lists dating from 1720. A take-over in 1991 meant transformation: obsolete winemaking equipment was thrown out, carefully selected wines bought-in. Beaune-Avaux is one of best reds.
Chanson Père & Fils Lighter-style reds, especially Beaune Clos des Fèves. Wines are aged in a 15th-century castle with walls several feet thick.
Joseph Drouhin Among the Burgundian elite. Wines of unreproachable quality, charming fruitiness, style and fine complexity.
Camille Giroud Craftsman-like firm with especially good reds. Some of the best are Les Cras, Teurons, Pommard Clos des Eveneaux and Cortons.
Louis Jadot American-owned big name since 1985, with strict quality policy, character, power and style.
Jaffelin Range of wines – Les Villages de Jaffelin – which are well priced from the lesser-known communes.
Louis Latour Family firm of high standing. Red wines are best from the company's own estate (eg Château Corton Grancey), but the white wines are generally of a higher quality.
Patriarche Père & Fils *Négociant* firm whose cellars are certainly worth a visit. Range includes generous, sturdy-tasting quality burgundies.
Domaine des Pierres Blanches Modest estate with white and red Cote de Beaune of excellent quality.

PLACES OF INTEREST

There is an 18-hole golf-course at Levernois and in Meursanges balloon trips can be booked at Château de Laborde. During the season, a sound and light show takes place in the courtyard of the Hôtel-Dieu. Find information at the Office du Tourisme or hotels. On Saturday there is a market in the town centre.

RELATED TO WINE

Across from Hôtel-Dieu, Patriarche Père & Fils and the Parisian publisher Flammarion have set up a unique documentation centre, the Athenaeum de la Vigne et du Vin. Exhibitions take place there, and the library has approximately 100,000 books about wine, Burgundy and gastronomy.

Left Beaune has many conveniently located bars and restaurants.

POMMARD

Pommard lies just 3.5 kilometres south of Beaune: leave on the N74 heading south and when the road splits, take the right fork (the D973) into the centre of Pommard.

The village is easily recognized by its spireless church. Vines almost completely cover the hills behind and to the south, although this has not always been the case, a fact belied by the name of one of Pommard's Premiers Crus, Les Epenots, named after the pine-tree wood which used to be there.

Pommard's good reputation for wine spans centuries. It was praised by Henry IV, Louis XV and Victor Hugo, while the 16th-century poet Ronsard wrote how wondrous it was '...that in such a small place such a great wine could be born'. A true Pommard has intense colour and power, and must age a long time before its initial toughness changes into velvety smoothness. Unfortunately not all satisfy this description; many are of uninspiring, average quality. However, Château de Pommard (open to visitors), with its walled 20-hectare vineyard, proves Pommard of village level can impress.

A busy road runs straight through the village. To the side of it is the surprisingly spacious church square, the heart of

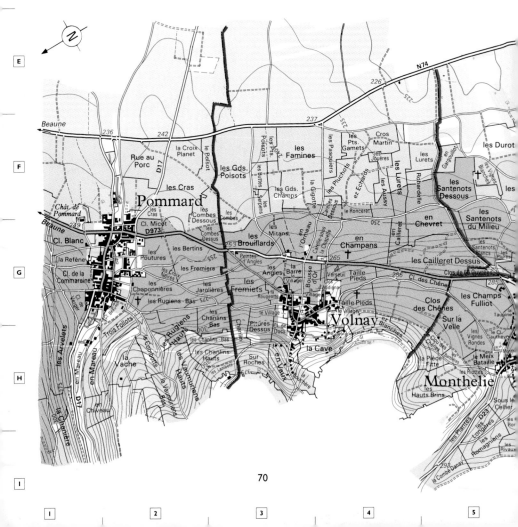

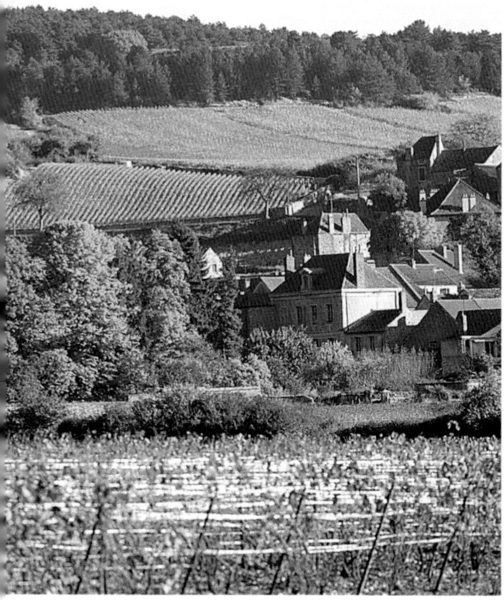

Left *Monthelie produces a red wine which is closer in style to that of its neighbour – Volnay. A tiny amount of white is also produced.*

Pommard

·· — ·· — ··	Commune (parish) or Canton boundary
━━	Commune Appellation boundary
▩	Premier Cru vineyard
▨	Commune Appellation vineyard
□	Other vineyard
✝	Vineyard part-owned by the Hospices de Beaune
⊡	Woods
═ 25 ═	Contour interval 5 metres
⁄	Internal vineyard boundary
▬	Wine route

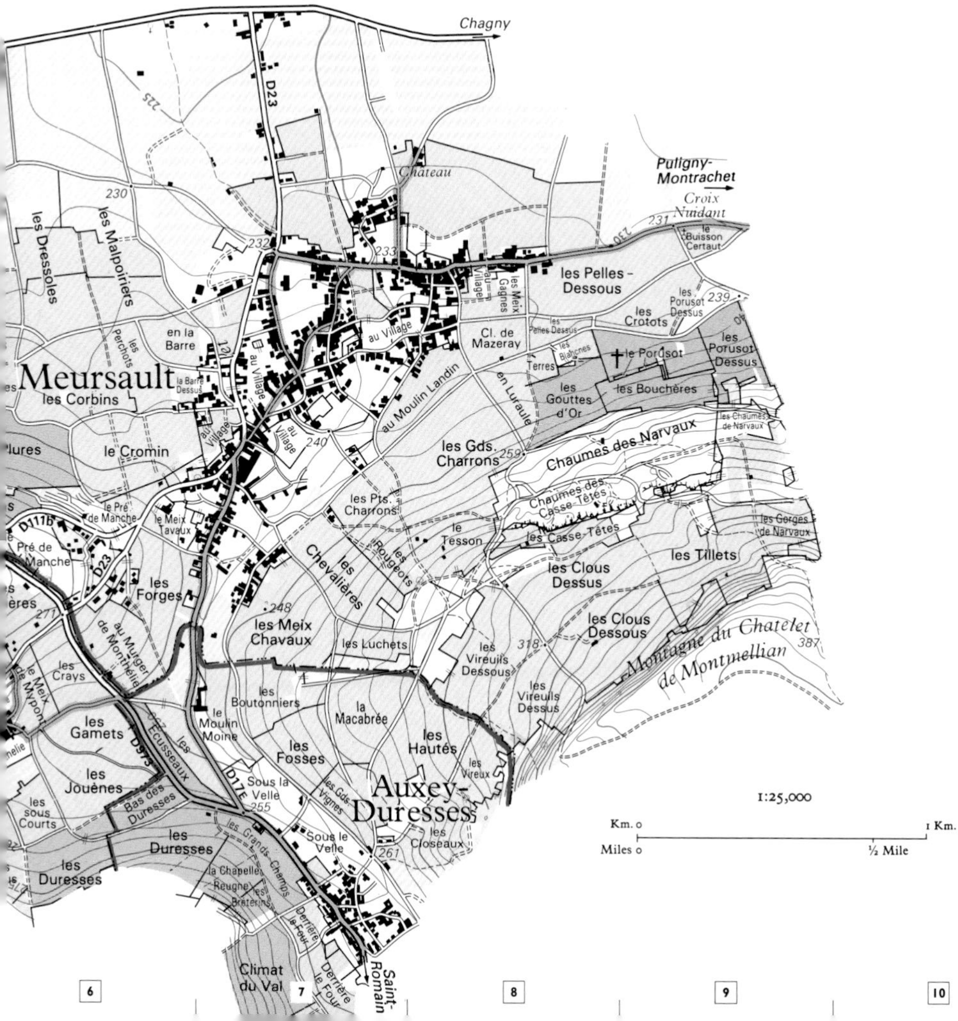

Chagny
D23
225
Chateau
Puligny-Montrachet
Croix Nuidant
231
230
le Buisson Certaut
les Dressoles
les Malpoiriers
232
233
les Pelles-Dessous
au Village
les Meix Gagnes
les Porusot Dessus
239
les Crotots
les Perchots
en la Barre
au Village
Cl. de Mazeray
les Pelles Dessus
les Blanches
le Porusot
les Porusot Dessus
Meursault
la Barre Dessus
les Corbins
au Village
Terres
les Gouttes d'Or
les Bouchères
au Moulin Landin
en Luraule
les Chaumes de Narvaux
les Cromin
au Village
240
les Gds. Charrons
259
Chaumes des Narvaux
le Pré de Manche
les Pts. Charrons
Chaumes des Casse-Têtes
D111b
Pré de Manche
le Meix Tavaux
le Tesson
les Casse-Têtes
les Gorges de Narvaux
D23
les Forges
les Rougeots
les Chevalières
les Clous Dessus
les Tillets
248
271
les Meix Chavaux
les Luchets
les Clous Dessous
au Murger de Monthelie
les Vireuils Dessous
318
Montagne du Chatelet de Montmellian
387
les Crays
le Meix de Mypont
les Boutonniers
les Vireuils Dessus
le Moulin Moine
la Macabrée
les Gamets
D973
les Ecusseaux
les Fosses
les Hautés
les Vireux
les Jouènes
D17E
Sous la Velle
255
les Gds. Vignes
Auxey-Duresses
Bas des Duresses
les sous Courts
les Duresses
les Grands-Champs
Sous le Velle
261
les Closeaux
la Chapelle
Reugne
les Bréterins
les Duresses
Derrière le Four
Climat du Val
Saint-Romain
1:25,000
Km. 0
1 Km.
Miles 0
½ Mile

POMMARD

RESTAURANT

Café du Pont
Tel: 80 22 03 41
Gastronomic delights such as *coq à la lie de vin* and *estouffade de boeuf bourguignon* are served for FF100 or less. Pommards from about FF120.

RECOMMENDED PRODUCERS

Comte Armand/Domaine du Clos des Epeneaux A top estate, easy to find near the church. The wines are intensely concentrated and need years of cellaring.

Domaine Michel Gaunoux A 'working museum', offering wines from recent years, and housing stock from the past decades. Concentrated Pommards, excellent with age.

Jean-Marc Boillot Excellent wines, including Premier Cru Montrevots.

Domaine de Mme Bernard de Coursel Cellar beneath a fine house on the square. Good Pommards: Grand Clos des Epenots and Rugiens.

Domaine Michel Ganoux High-quality concentrated Pommards.

Domaine Lejeune Perfect Pommards, foot trodden in truly traditional manner, with fruit, charm and enough backbone to develop in bottle.

Domaine Mussy Traditional estate, distinctive wines: power and complexity.

Domaine Parent Reliable, expertly made wines. Legend has it that Thomas Jefferson was guided by a Parent on his Burgundy visit in 1787 and from him bought wine for the White House.

Château de Pommard Beautifully renovated property. The wines are sublime – and expensive.

PLACES OF INTEREST

A low, white, stone cross – the 'croix de Pommard' – southeast of the village marks the spot of a once fordable point in the Dheune River. It took on special meaning in the expression *Tu n'est pas encore à la croix de Pommard;* ('You are not at the end of your problems yet'.)

VOLNAY

RESTAURANTS

Le Cellier Volnaysien
Tel: 80 21 61 04
Near to the church. One of the dining rooms is an arched cellar. Authentic regional dishes (*oeufs en meurette, jambon persillé, coq à la lie*). Various wines, including a range of Volnays, are served by the glass. Starts at FF100.

the village. There are wood-carvings to be seen in the church itself, which dates from the 18th century. Some of the streets in Pommard are only four metres wide, a reminder of the days of the stage-coach. There is an interesting wine shop called Les Domaines de Pommard, situated opposite the post office which stocks wines from more than 20 producers.

VOLNAY

Leaving Pommard travelling south on the D973, take the fork off to the right and up-hill through the Premier Cru vineyards surrounding Volnay. The vineyards of Les Brouillards and Les Angles are on the left, Frémiets on the right.

Volnay nestles against a steep slope and looks down on Pommard. At its north it is marked by a tasting centre and a giant bottle. There is also a 16th-century chapel which is all that remains of a castle built by the first duke of Burgundy. Most of the houses date from the 17th and 18th centuries.

Volnay's Romanesque church is actually 14th-century and has recently been completely restored, thanks to donations from the inhabitants. By following a path leading upwards behind the church (there is a signpost 'panorama' pointing the way), you will find a delightful vantage point. On clear days you can even see Mont Blanc from here.

Volnay's red wine has enjoyed fame for centuries. Records show that, as early as the 6th century it was served in Italy and in 1328 at the crowning of Philippe de Valois in Reims. After the conquest of Burgundy in 1477 Louis XI confiscated the entire harvest. Louis XIV and XV were also enthusiasts.

These are among the Côte de Beaune's finest red wines. They are striking for their elegance, soft taste, perfect balance and delicate bouquet. The best come from Premiers Crus Caillerets, Champans, Clos de la Bousse d'Or, Clos des Chênes and Clos des Ducs. Wines from Premier Cru vineyard Clos des Santenots bear the name Volnay but, strictly speaking, this vineyard is in the commune of Meursault.

MONTHELIE

Leaving Volnay on the D973, turn right (south) and you will pass on your left the Grand Cru vineyards of Champans and Cailleret Dessus. After a while, the road splits. Take the right fork, follow the hillside round and you will reach Monthelie.

Two multicoloured spires dominate the skyline: the highest is 12th-century Romanesque, the other belongs to Château de Monthelie. Monthelie boasts buildings from the 16th, 17th and 18th centuries, most inhabited by winegrowers.

In 1855 a Dr Lavalle wrote that Monthelie wines were worth only three-quarters Volnay's. What he meant was they resemble Volnays, with similar grace, but were rustic and somewhat softer. The price does indeed tend to reflect that.

Auberge des Vignes
Tel: 80 22 24 48
Pleasant rustic restaurant with affordable well-prepared regional dishes and attractive wines.

RECOMMENDED PRODUCERS

Domaine du Marquis d'Angerville Very fine and often velvety Volnays, such as Champans and Clos des Ducs.
Domaine Yvon Clerget One of Europe's oldest family estates (1268). Volnays are elegant and firm.
Bernard Glantenay Delicious Volnays: charming, supple and fruity. Dependable wines at good prices.
Domaine Michel Lafarge Top wines of colour, roundness, distinction.
Hubert de Montille Great traditionally-made wines, stern when young, softening after six to ten years.
Domaine de la Pousse d'Or Cellars beneath a stately mansion. Sublime, refined and balanced Volnays.

MONTHELIE

RECOMMENDED PRODUCERS

Denis Boussey Consistently good, especially Premier Cru Champs Fulliots.
Château de Monthelie Wine to withstand any criticism: Premier Cru with grace, firmness with hints of vanilla.

PLACES OF INTEREST

The name is pronounced 'Mont'lie'. Its many owners have included the monastery of Cluny, and a pharmacist from Beaune who bought it in its entirety in 1730.

The heritage of this part of the Côte de Beaune is steeped in wine:
Far left Gateway of the Château les Communs in Pommard.
Left Château de Pommard's cellar with its intricate wrought iron door.
Above Example of a stone plaque incorporating a bunch of grapes in the design (Pommard).

AUXEY-DURESSES

RESTAURANT

La Crémaillière
Tel: 80 21 22 60
In a chic interior you can enjoy regional specialities and local wines. There is usually a menu offered at under FF100; the next price is almost twice as much. The quality of the food is good and usually a few inexpensive wines are available which are not on the wine list.

RECOMMENDED PRODUCERS

Gérard Creusefond
Strong, dependable red wines.

Jean-Pierre Diconne
Owns some of the Premier Cru Les Duresses and makes rustic reds and sometimes excellent whites. There is always a warm welcome here but quality can vary greatly from one bottle to the next so choose carefully.

Henri Latour
Modern equipment is used here to make fruity, expressive wines, including red Auxey-Duresses and Bourgogne Hautes-Côtes de Beaune.

Leroy
An almost legendary small firm which has made a speciality of thoroughly matured wines. In the cellars (situated next to the Watteau River, not far from the church) lie thousands of bottles of Burgundy's oldest and finest vintages. Quality is top priority here, but prices are extremely high.

Michel Prunier
Superior wines from a small estate with modern equipment. Try the red Auxey-Duresses Clos du Val (which needs quite a few years' bottle-age) and the exquisite white Auxey-Duresses.

Roy Frères
With nearly 11 hectares, this is one of the largest properties in the district. Not all the wines are consistently successful, but the red Auxey-Duresses is reliable.

AUXEY-DURESSES

Leave Monthelie and head towards the D973. Turn right onto this road, travelling west towards Auxey-Duresses. Auxey-le-Petit and Melin also make up part of this commune.

The most important place in Auxey-Duresses is the church, whose clock tower has been declared a monument. Inside there is a triptych with depictions from the life of the Holy Virgin. The weather-beaten, grey chapel of Auxey-le-Petit is also worth a visit. On the plateau of Mont Mélian, below Auxey-Duresses, are the remains of a prehistoric settlement.

Due to its difficult name, sometimes rather reserved taste and modest production, red Auxey-Duresses is mostly sold simply as Côte de Beaune-Villages. The whites have more charm and quality, but less than half as much is made. The reds come from the west- and southwest-facing vineyards adjoining Volnay, while the whites come predominantly from the other side of the valley, closer to Meursault.

Right The appreciation of wine in Burgundy can be surprisingly straightforward, even for the region's finest wines.

SAINT-ROMAIN

A narrow, winding road leads from Auxey-Duresses to Saint-Romain, which has a high and low part: Saint-Romain-le-Haut situated a few dozen metres above Saint-Romain-le-Bas.

The upper village attracts quite a few visitors on Sunday afternoons as a local society has set out a nice walking track around the remains of the castle. The ruins themselves are not particularly impressive, but the views are wonderful.

A well-known barrel-maker, François Frères, lives here. He supplies the Domaine de la Romanée Conti, the Hospices de Beaune, Domaine Leflaive and wineries in California and Oregon. If you look down the hill from le-Haut, you can see his oak staves stored in piles to weather.

Also in the higher village is a 15th-century church with a Romanesque tower, a sloping nave and a sculpted pulpit dating from 1619. Archeological finds from the surrounding caves, prove people have lived near Saint-Romain since prehis-

ST-ROMAIN

RESTAURANT

Hôtel-Restaurant Les Roches
Tel: 80 21 21 63
The service, in this country hotel, is friendly and the menus (starting at about FF100) consist of regional dishes (*coq au vin, poulet de Bresse aux morilles et à la crème*). There are a few simple rooms available.

RECOMMENDED PRODUCERS

Domaine Henri et Gilles Buisson
Average-sized wine estate with more than a dozen hectares, not only in St-Romain, but also in six other communes of the Côte de Beaune. The white and red wines are of good average quality.
Bernard Fèvre
Small property: reliable red St-Romain.
Alain Gras
Situated in St-Romian-le-Haut, this estate produces white and red wines with fruit, freshness and charm.
Taupenot Père & Fils
Locally this is the fifth largest estate. Very decent red and soft, fresh white St-Romain and Auxey-Duresses. The cellars store over 100,000 bottles from the last ten vintages.
Domaine René Thévenin-Monthelie & Fils
Delicious wines of great charm, such as the white and red St-Romain, red Monthelie and red Beaune.

MEURSAULT

 HOTELS

Les Arts
Tel: 80 21 20 28
Spartan rooms, creaking floors, loud water pipes: a simple country hotel for guests who sleep soundly. Prices from about FF120. You can also eat well and inexpensively here.

Les Charmes
Tel: 80 21 63 53
Two styles of rooms here: light and modern or classic – all tastefully furnished. Friendly reception. Swimming pool. Prices at about FF400.

Les Magnolias
Tel: 80 21 23 23
Beautiful hotel in renovated, 18th-century building opposite Domaine Prieur. 12 rooms (starting at FF350).

Le Mont Mélian
Tel: 80 21 64 90
In the centre of Mersault. 12 light, quite rustic rooms with bathrooms. Free bicycles and maps of local cycling routes. Prices about FF250.

RESTAURANTS

Hôtel du Centre
Tel: 80 21 20 75
Affordable, regional dishes. The menus begin under FF100. Also has a few rooms available.

Relais de la Diligence
Tel: 80 21 21 32
A large restaurant, a few kilometres from the village centre, on the other side of the *route nationale*, offering a variety of menus. The second most inexpensive is very good value at about FF120, which includes dishes such as *aiguillette de boeuf à la moutarde ancienne*.

Above Meursault produces highly distinctive white wines. Surprisingly, none of its vineyards has been recognized as a Grand Cru despite the often unsurpassable level of quality from the top Premiers Crus. Left Traditional wicker paniers used to be used for the harvest. Buckets or plastic paniers are now used, being kinder to the grapes.

Right The ancient art of cooperage remains a highly respected craft. This cooper, based in Saint-Romain, has illustrious clients from all over the world.

toric times. The town hall houses a small exhibition of them.

This was practically a forgotten wine village until Roland Thévenin became mayor. His promotional activities included exhibiting wines at the exchange in Dijon in 1962 under the theme 'Mon Village'. For a long time this was used on labels, folders and signposts. You still see it on a few road signs.

The red wines of Saint-Romain belong to the lighter types of burgundy and commonly have a fruity, cherry-like taste and agreeable suppleness. Again, the white is not especially full, but it certainly has plenty of fresh, juicy fruit and is in general somewhat higher in quality than the red.

MEURSAULT

To reach Meursault you need to retrace your steps through Auxey-Duresses on the D973. Then, where the road forks, take the right turn (the D17E) into Meursault.

Anyone visiting Meursault can see immediately that its a wine village, by the signs the winegrowers hang on the front of their houses. Nearly every building along the long street that leads out of the village towards Puligny is decorated in this way. This is typical of Meursault – it is one of the most energetic villages of the Côte d'Or, holding many wine events, including the Paulée de Meursault on the third Monday in November: a six-course afternoon meal in the *cuverie* of Château de Meursault. There is a similar festival and tasting session in September, the Banée de Meursault.

White wines are in the majority here – there are ten times as many as reds – and it is these that have given Meursault international fame. They have a fine, almost buttery taste, hints of ripe, sun-drenched fruits, nuts and toasted bread, and the acidity to remain fresh for decades. Meursault has no Grand Cru vineyards – the best wines come from six Premier Cru sites: Les Perrières, Les Genièvres, Les Poruzots, Les Charmes (the largest), La Goutte d'Or and Les Bouchères.

The Château de Meursault is the main feature here. It has a wine-theme art exhibition, and gives plenty of opportunity to taste its marvellous wines. There is another castle in the the village. It has a fine multicoloured roof and today functions as the town hall. It looks out over the 14th-century Eglise Saint-Nicolas, with its striking, Gothic spire.

RECOMMENDED PRODUCERS

Robert Ampeau et Fils Leading estate, with stylish wines of intense fruit and elegant balance: Meursault, Puligny-Montrachet, Beaune, Pommard and Savigny-lès-Beaune.

Raymond Ballot-Millot & Fils Fairly large estate with some 20 high quality wines, including 5 Meursaults (brilliant Premiers Crus), 2 white Chassagne-Montrachets, 3 Pommards.

Pierre Boillot Excellent white Charmes and red Volnay Santenots.

A Buisson-Battault Owns land in four Premiers Crus: excellent wines, very good ordinary Meursault.

Domaine des Comtes Lafon Painstakingly nurtured wines: both the white (6 Meursaults and a Montrachet), and reds (3 Volnays) are near perfect.

François Jobard Aristocratic wines, leanly refined in youth, maturing very slowly. Buy here only if you have a cool cellar to store them in for years.

Château de Meursault Wines made at the castle: excellent quality; even ordinary burgundies are delightful.

Michelot-Buisson Classic Meursaults. Various family members have their own labels.

Raymond Millot & Fils Attractive Meursaults, full of nuances. Also a good Puligny-Montrachet.

Domaine Jean Monnier et Fils Beautiful, rather firm Meursaults with a slightly nutty taste, and a hint of toast in the aftertaste.

Domaine René Monnier Extensive estate with excellent red and white wines. The whites need bottle-age to lose some of their acidity.

Pierre Morey Great wines with wonderful bouquet, great complexity: Bâtard-Montrachet, Meursault-Perrières, Meursault-Tessons, Meursault.

Domaine Jacques Prieur Many Côte d'Or gems: Chambertin, Chambertin-Clos de Bèze, Musigny, Clos de Vougeot, Volnay Santenots, Meursaults-Perrières, Puligny-Montrachet – Les Combettes, Chevalier-Montrachet, Montrachet.

Ropiteau Frères *Négociant* with tasting cellars in Meursault itself and offices beside the *route nationale*.

PLACES OF INTEREST

The hamlet of l'Hôpital de Meursault (along the *route nationale*) is organized well for visitors, with tasting rooms and hospitable restaurants. Its name derives from a leper colony founded in 1180 whose portal, though now half buried, can still be seen. There is also a weekly market on Fridays.

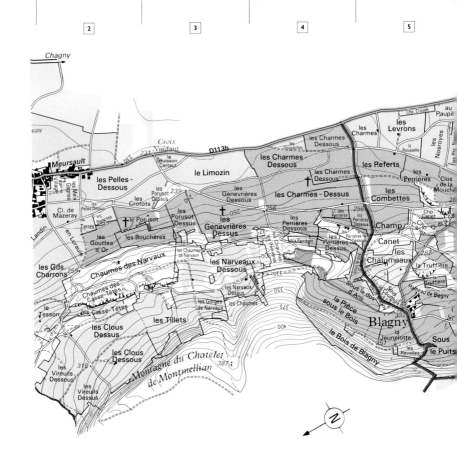

Map labels: Chagny · Croix Niudaut · Meursault · les Pelles-Dessous · le Limozin · les Charmes-Dessous · les Charmes Dessous · les Charmes-Dessus · les Referts · les Perrières · Clos de la Mouche · les Combettes · les Levrons · les Charmes · au Paupil · les Nosroyes · le Buisson Certaut · les Porusot Dessus · les Crotots · Cl. de Mazeray · les Genevrières Dessous · les Genevrières Dessus · le Porusot · les Porusot Dessus · les Perrières Dessous · les Perrières Dessus · Champ Canet · Canet · les Chalumeaux · la Truffière · les Gouttes d'Or · les Bouchères · les Chaumes de Narvaux · les Narvaux Dessous · les Gds. Charrons · Chaumes des Narvaux · Chaumes des Casse-Têtes · les Narvaux Dessus · Sous le dos d'Âne · la Pièce sous le Bois · Hameau de Blagny · le Tesson · les Casse-Têtes · les Gorges de Narvaux · les Chaumes · les Tillets · le Bois de Blagny · Blagny · la Jeunelotte · les Clous Dessous · Montagne du Chatelet de Montmellian · les Ravelles · Sous le Puits · les Vireuls Dessous · les Vireuls Dessus

PULIGNY-MONTRACHET

Drive south out of Meursault on the D113b and, after about two kilometres, passing Premier Cru vineyards Les Charmes Dessous and les Charmes Dessus, you will arrive in Puligny.

Without prior knowledge no one would suspect that Puligny-Montrachet produces some of the world's greatest and most expensive white wines because the village itself has no allure. Its ordinary streets come out onto two squares and the only notable building is Château de Puligny-Montrachet (visitors are welcome and wine can be tasted). The village church is worth a brief visit for its marvellous choir stalls.

But despite its rather plain appearance, no trip can be complete without visiting this village. The true greatness of Puligny-Montrachet is not found above ground, but in the soil, which is perfectly suited for the Chardonnay grape. Natural factors result in a truly brilliant white wine, aromatic, full of peach and apricot fruit flavours and great complexity. Alexandre Dumas (1802–70) believed that top wine, Le Montrachet, should be drunk 'on your knees and with bared head'; another compared the bouquet to singing in a Gothic cathedral; in fact nobody disputes its place today as potentially the greatest white wine of Burgundy. It should never be drunk before it has aged at least eight years in bottle.

The Le Montrachet vineyard is marked by small gates, and is surrounded by the village's three other Grand Cru

Below *Chassagne Montrachet and the similarly unassuming-looking Puligny-Montrachet produce some of the world's most glamorous wines.*

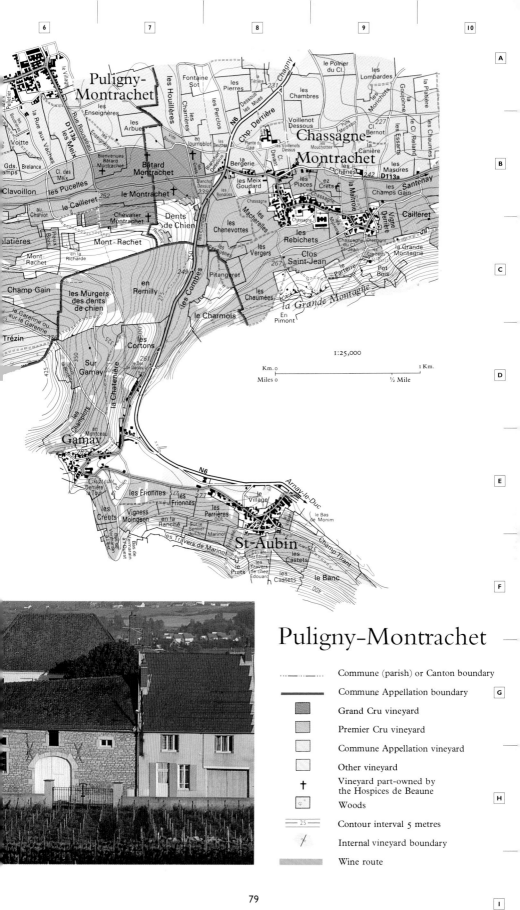

Puligny-Montrachet

Commune (parish) or Canton boundary

Commune Appellation boundary

Grand Cru vineyard

Premier Cru vineyard

Commune Appellation vineyard

Other vineyard

+ Vineyard part-owned by the Hospices de Beaune

Woods

Contour interval 5 metres

Internal vineyard boundary

Wine route

PULIGNY-MONTRACHET

RESTAURANT

Le Montrachet
Tel: 80 21 30 06
Regional and inventive modern dishes
from about FF200. Also a marvellous
collection of burgundies and often
terrific Aligoté. Rooms too (30), with
old rustic furniture, from about FF475.

RECOMMENDED PRODUCERS

Louis Carillon & Fils In Puligny
since 1632, with cellars in a house of
stones from the old château. History
has it that, during the revolution, the

curé of Puligny hid here: his makeshift
confessional and his escape route still
remain. Expertly run estate with
excellent Puligny-Montrachet Premiers
Crus.
Chartron et Trébuchet A *négociant*
founded in 1984, which has strict
quality controls for its excellent
Grand Cru vineyard sites.
Domaine Leflaive The most
respected Puligny-Montrachet estate.
White wines of rich complexity, style
and sensuality. The range includes
Montrachets, marvellous Premiers
Crus, an excellent commune wine
and an attractive red Blagny.
Olivier Leflaive Frères Small,
successful *négociant* founded due to
demand for Leflaive wines becoming
greater than supply. The solution was
to buy grapes in from other growers
and vinify and mature them.
Domaine Etienne Sauzet Sublime
whites with depth and distinction:
among the very best of the village.

sites: Chevalier-, Bâtard- and Bienvenues-Bâtard-Montrachet.
The first of these produces wines famous for their finesse
and elegance. The second for richer, fatter wines. The third
for less weighty but still amazingly complex wines.

Nestling above Puligny-Montrachet is the hamlet of Blagny.
The walk there is very pleasant, with a fine view of Puligny
as well as Meursault on arrival. Blagny is also surrounded by
Premier Cru vineyards, giving slightly more austere wines.

CHASSAGNE-MONTRACHET

The peace of present day Chassagne-Montrachet belies its
bloody history. In the 15th century, John of Chalon, Prince
of Orange, decided to oppose Louis XI. As a result, the king
proclaimed that the prince must hang and that all his pos-
sessions should be burnt. After a series of skirmishes, John
retreated to the château of Chassagne, then had to flee for
safety, abandoning Chassagne unprotected. The king's soldiers began to plunder and murder, and the village and its
château went up in flames. The inhabitants thus received the
nickname 'the crushed'. Here and there, among the narrow,
winding streets, you can still find an old well or a part of a
wall from the vanished castle.

The village of Chassagne added the name of its most
famous vineyard to its own on the same day as neighbouring Puligny did the same. Thus, on November 27, 1879,
Chassagne became Chassagne-Montrachet. It also owns part

Far left *The neat lines of a vineyard in Puligny-Montrachet.* Left *Old buildings, such as this, evoke the timelessness of the area.*

CHASSAGNE MONTRACHET

RECOMMENDED PRODUCERS

Domaine Guy Amiot-Bonfils Try the white Chassagne les Caillerets and les Vergers, the white Puligny les Demoiselles, the red Chassagne les Clos St-Jean and majestic Montrachet.
Blain-Gagnard Small estate with distinguished Caillerets, Morgeot, Criots-Bâtard-Montrachet, Bâtard-Montrachet and Montrachet.
Jean-Noël Gagnard A prime source for great white burgundies.
Marc Morey Pure white burgundies with an elegant firmness. The red Caillerets is also delicious.
Michel Niellon Sublime, but rare Grands Crus and splendid Les Vergers.
Paul Pillot Sumptuously appealing fruity white Premiers Crus.
Domaine Ramonet Top property in Chassagne: fantastic whites, from local to Montrachet, and exceptional red Clos de la Boudriotte and Clos St-Jean.

of Bâtard-Montrachet and all of tiny Grand Cru, Criots-Bâtard-Montrachet.

Besides these Grands Crus, which produce brilliant, richly concentrated, complex white wines, the wines from the Premiers Crus of this commune can also offer impressive depth and distinction.

In contrast to Puligny, Chassagne produces more red than white wine, and, if they do not reach the exalted level of the whites, Chassagne reds can be richly coloured, smooth-drinking wines of quality.

SAINT-AUBIN AND GAMAY

Follow the D113b west out of Puligny-Montrachet, turn south (past the Grands Crus vines of Bâtard- and le Montrachet) to the N6; head right for St-Aubin.

Saint-Aubin's central feature is its church, with its striking, grey-stoned clock tower, and there is also a castle (built in 1850) now used as a cellar for maturing wines.

White Saint-Aubins have an agreeable hazelnut aroma and soft freshness with, occasionally, some finesse. They are a good-quality alternative to more expensive burgundies. Reds tend to be firm with a touch of rustic earthiness.

If you keep going through the village you will reach the hamlet of Gamay, dominated by the weather-beaten, grey château of the Seigneur Du May, who, legend says, brought back from the crusades the Gamay grape.

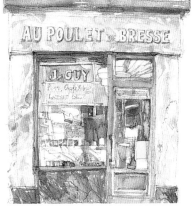

ST AUBIN

RECOMMENDED PRODUCERS

Jean-Claude Bachelet In Gamay, this small producer makes showpiece Bienvenues-Bâtard-Montrachet.
Raoul Clerget Distinctive white St-Aubin Le Charmois and white and red St-Aubin Les Frionnes.
Marc Colin Gamay grower with delicious white Premiers Crus from St-Aubin and Chassagne-Montrachet, also Le Montrachet.

SANTENAY

There are two roads that lead south out of Chassagne-Montrachet. You can take either to reach Santenay. You will pass the Premier Cru vineyards of Chassagne-Montrachet: Les Fairendes and Les Petits Clos on the right and Morgeot on the left; and then the Premier Cru vineyards belonging to Santenay: Les Gravières and Passetemps on the right, and on the hillside behind, La Comme and Beauregard.

Just like Chassagne-Montrachet, Santenay is made up of a higher and a lower village part, although these two are much further away from each other. The first part you come to is Santenay-le-Bas, which is the largest part of the village.

Before it was famous for its wine, Santenay was better known for its water; medicinal spring waters were found here in Roman times and are still used today. In fact the village was formerly called Santenay-les-Bains. It is said that the water has healing qualities, helping rheumatism, among others things. Because of this, it has the status of a health resort and, under an idiosyncratic French law, it is therefore allowed a casino! Thus Santenay has the only gambling palace in the whole of the Côte d'Or.

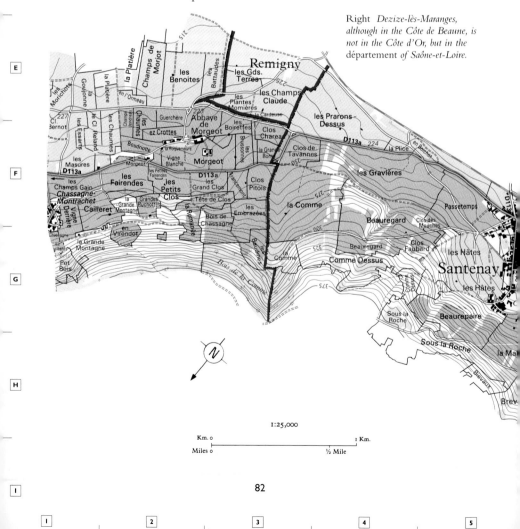

Right *Dezize-lès-Maranges, although in the Côte de Beaune, is not in the Côte d'Or, but in the département of Saône-et-Loire.*

1:25,000

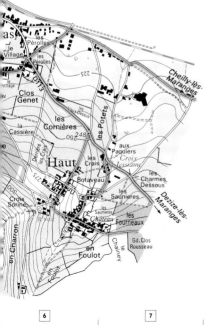

Santenay

·—·—·—	Commune (parish) or Canton boundary
——	Commune Appellation boundary
▢	Premier Cru vineyard
▢	Commune Appellation vineyard
▢	Other vineyard
▢	Woods
═ 25 ═	Contour interval 5 metres
/	Internal vineyard boundary
▨▨▨	Wine route

SANTENAY

RESTAURANTS

L'Ouillette
Tel: 80 20 62 34
An established name in Santenay.
People from the village and its
surroundings come to enjoy regional
dishes such as fillet of perch in Aligoté
sauce, *coq au vin* and *entrecôte grillée*.
Menus from about FF75.

Le Terroir
Tel: 80 20 63 47
Next to L'Ouillette, on the village
square. Pleasant interior, good service
and dishes somewhat less conventional
than its neighbour's. Thus there is
always a fresh fish of the day, and
sometimes pasta. Menu prices start at
about FF85 on week-day lunchtimes.

RECOMMENDED PRODUCERS

Domaine Josep Belland One
of the laregest and most important
local producers. The red wines are
often supple and juicy and the
white Criots-Bâtard-Montrachet is
excellent.
Michel Clair Well-respected,
sturdily-structured wines.

Vincent Girardin Medium-sized,
dynamically-run estate. The show-
piece wine is the exclusive Clos de la
Confrérie. The Santenay Premier Cru
Maladière is also highly praiseworthy.
There are also glorious whites, eg the
Chassagne-Morgeot and the luscious
Savigny-lès-Beaune-Les Vermots with
its complex wood flavours.
Jessiaume Père & Fils Traditional
wines, powerful and rich in tannin.
Domaine Lequin-Rousset Award-
winning reds, offering good balance
between fruit and tannin.

In Santenay-le-Bas you can visit two interesting castles.
Château Philippe le Hardi derives its name from the first
duke of Burgundy (Philip the Bold) and has a massive, 14th-
century tower. It houses a wine museum and wine is made
in its ultra-modern *cuverie*. Not far from the large village
square is the Château du Passe-Temps. Its cellars go down as
deep as ten metres and are the largest of the Côte d'Or.

Santenay-le-Haut is just one kilometre away and there is
a pleasant walk through gently sloping vineyards to reach it.
Close by is the hamlet of Saint-Jean.

Directly behind Saint-Jean rise the steep cliffs which sur-
round the entire commune on the west side. In fact the
underlying geology of this part of the Côte is complex with
faults breaking up the smooth sequence of the strata.
Consequently the soil in Santenay is very varied, enabling it
to produce many different styles of wine, mostly red.
According to a local saying, the best vineyards of the commune lie 'east of the belfry' and it is there that most of the
Premiers Crus are found – Les Gravières, La Comme and
Clos de Tavanne. Les Gravières, with its heavy, stony soil is
the best known, while Clos de Tavanne has a name for solid,

reserved wines. La Comme, further up the slope, has lighter soil and produces a correspondingly lighter style wine.

Red Santenay is a rather reserved burgundy style with firm structure, modest finesse and complexity. Some of the wines can be excellent and mature into fine bottles.

MARANGES

As you travel up from Santenay to the Hautes-Côtes, you will pass through at least two of the three villages which make up the appellation of Maranges. Created in 1989, this appellation sits just outside the *département* of Côte d'Or, but still belongs to the wine district of the same name. The villages are (north to south) Dezize-lès-Maranges, Sampigny-lès-Maranges and Cheilly-lès-Maranges.

The small village of Dezize is clustered around a crossroads and its pretty Romanesque church lies close by. The road from here winds downwards to Sampigny-lès-Maranges which nestles in a small, wooded valley, fringed by dramatic rock formations – more and more of them as you travel south. Cheilly-lès-Maranges, stretching out across the low hills, is surrounded by vineyards and lush pastures. The hamlet of Mercey, a few kilometres away, also belongs to this commune.

The best Maranges wines, mainly red, are strong-flavoured with good colour and fruit (they were once used to beef up lighter Côtes de Beaune-Villages blends). They can be of good quality and are generally reasonably priced.

Far left A traditional vertical press. Horizontal pneumatic presses are nowadays used which tend to be more gentle on the grapes.

Left and above Images of Santenay and Maranges; communes producing a range of generally reasonably priced wines.

Prosper Maufoux Expertly managed wine establishment on the village square and owned, since 1994, by an American importer, Robert Fairchild. Its white wines generally are of better quality than the reds. Its Clos des Gravières is delicious.

Jean Moreau/Domaine de la Buissière One of the best producers of Santenay. Well-rounded reds with colour, tannin, fruit and suppleness – try the Santenay-Clos des Mouches.

Mestre Père & Fils Large property with distinctive red wines from various Santenay Premiers Crus as well as wines from other communes.

Domaine Prieur-Brunet Juicy, supple red wines and fine white Premiers Crus from Meursault. The cellars (with a small wine museum) are also worth the visit.

MARANGES

RECOMMENDED PRODUCERS

Domaine Bachelet & Ses Fils (Dezize) Large estate – the largest owner of Maranges Premiers Crus – with 20 different wines, from both the Côte de Beaune and the Côte de Nuits. Fruity reds are usually good.

La Cave de Cheilly (Cheilly) Next to the Canal du Centre and the D974, this estate produces engaging wines including a Maranges Premier Cru. Visitors can watch a video presentation showing the estate.

Maurice Charleux (Dezize) Traditional estate. Fresh, red wines.

Domaine du Château de Mercey (Cheilly) A respected estate with fresh white wines (Aligoté, Hautes-Côtes de Beaune and Mercurey) and smooth, refined reds (Hautes-Côtes de Beaune, Mercurey and Santenay). Part-owned by Antonin Rodet in Mercurey who is currently carrying out much experimentation to improve the wines.

Domaine Fernand Chevrot (Cheilly) Situated in a large farm above the village, this is a fine source of modestly-priced, attractive red and white wines, including Cheilly-lès-Maranges and Santenay-Clos Rousseau. It has a fine 18th-century cellar and you are sure to experience a friendly welcome.

Yvon et Chantal Contat-Grangé (Dezize) This couple come from Annecy in Haute Savoie. They started renting their vines in 1980 and now have a modern business with fine red and white Maranges.

René Martin (Cheilly) Although situated in Cheilly, Martin makes a flavoursome red wine from Sampigny.

HAUTES-COTES DE BEAUNE

The vineyards of the Hautes-Côtes de Beaune lie on the hillside slopes above the Côte d'Or just south of Beaune. Here, instead of the well-regimented lines of immaculately pruned vines, you see the rather spindly, more untidy Aligoté and Gamay grape varieties which are more suited to the less hospitable soil and climate here. The grapes ripen quicker in the Hautes-Côtes de Beaune than in the Hautes-Côtes de Nuits, and the resulting wines are somewhat sturdier.

To visit the charming villages of the Hautes-Côtes takes only half a day, although there are many delightful picnic spots if you can afford a more leisurely pace. From Santenay you can follow the signs up to small villages such as Dezize-lès-Maranges and then to the top of the Montagne des Trois Croix where there are stunning views of the Côte d'Or and Chalonnais. From here the road continues through the villages of Sampigny-lès-Maranges and Change, then on towards Nolay.

This is the quieter, less commercial side of Burgundy. Extremely rural, time seems to matter less here and prices for the wines are much more reasonable than further down

Below *A view of La Rochepot, the main town of the Hautes-Côtes. It is worth visiting if only to see its magnificent castle.*

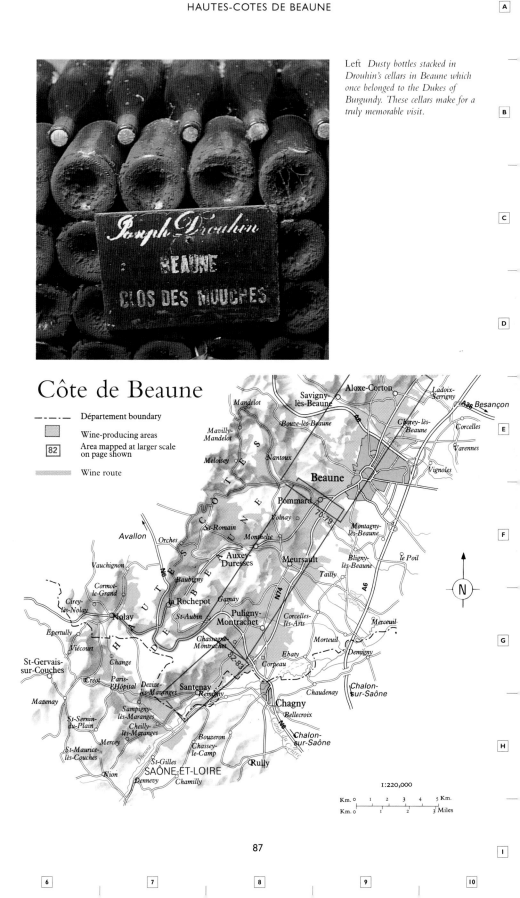

Left *Dusty bottles stacked in Drouhin's cellars in Beaune which once belonged to the Dukes of Burgundy. These cellars make for a truly memorable visit.*

Côte de Beaune

–·–·–·– Département boundary

Wine-producing areas

82 Area mapped at larger scale on page shown

Wine route

1:220,000

Km. 0 1 2 3 4 5 Km.
Km. 0   1   2   3 Miles

Views of La Rochepot: the Café de France in the town centre and picking blackcurrants (left) near the château, for the production of Crème de Cassis.

the hillside. Change is a pretty village with its oak-beamed market hall being particularly appealing. Nolay is also charming: half-timbered houses, a church with a striking stone spire and a 14th-century market hall (Place Monge). Nearby is the statue of Lazare Carnot, 'the organizer of the conquest' during the French Revolution. Not far from the village is the spectacular Gorge du Bout du Monde, at the end of the ravine Falaises de Cormot. Here dramatic sheer cliffs look down over a stream running along the valley floor and a spectacular 30-metre waterfall. To get there, you can take a road from Nolay which runs north to Vauchignon and the ravine.

From Nolay the D973 continues to La Rochepot, dominated by the magnificent Château de la Rochepot. Built in the 15th century, this was almost totally destroyed during the revolution, and was fully restored in the original style by the French president, Sadi Carnot, last century. It has six pepper pot towers, a Chinese room and a Gothic chapel. Near the entrance, a local farmer offers his wines to be tasted.

The route now continues to Orches, a village set against a stunning backdrop of dramatic rock formations. From the top of the cliff here, if the weather is good, you can look down on the village of Saint-Romain, the valley leading down to Meursault, the plain of the Saône, the Jura Mountains and, if it is a very clear day, Mont Blanc. Here also, above the village, is a small well with a few Gallic-Roman gravestones nearby. Grape growers at Orches make a quite pleasant, delicate rosé wine as well as Poire William distilled from fruit grown in the local orchards.

Now take the narrow road to the winegrowers' village of Meloisey with its monumental church tower. Follow the road to Mavilly-Mandelot and Mandelot with its 16th-century castle. Finally, head towards Pommard, with a stop in Nantoux known for its good wines and its 15th-century church.

HAUTES COTES DE BEAUNE

RESTAURANTS

Chez Denise
Tel: 80 21 70 38 (Evelle)
In the hamlet of Evelle, not far from Orches, Denise Lagelée cooks in a homely way; tasty regional dishes in an unpretentious, cosy ambiance. All this can be had for less than FF100 a menu. An address to cherish.

Hôtel Sainte-Marie
Tel: 80 21 73 19 (Nolay)
Country dishes, including *jambon persillé* and *oeufs en meurette*. Friendly service. Also hotel, but can be noisy.

RECOMMENDED PRODUCERS

Domaine François Charles & Fils (Nantoux) In the centre of the village: good wines, not only from the Hautes-Côtes, but also a Beaune Les Epenottes and a Volnay Les Fremiets.
Guillemard Dupont & Ses Fils (Meloisey) Wines of above-average quality, some whites bottled *sur lie*.
Domaine Fouquerand Père & Fils (La Rochepot) At the foot of the local castle: good red and white Hautes-Côtes de Beaune, as well as Volnays and a Santenay-Comme.
Domaine Lucien Jacob (Echevronne) Large, sound estate with red Hautes-Côtes de Beaune, Savigny-lès-Beaune, Savigny-Vergelesses.
Domaine Joliot (Nantoux) Mainly reds, although whites, eg Aligoté, also have merit. The Hautes-Côtes de Beaune often has a blackcurrant aroma and the Beaune Boucherottes and Pommard are worth tasting.
Mazilly Père & Fils (Meloisey) Mazilly is a dynamic figure here; he makes three kinds of red and a lovely Beaune Les Vignes Franches.
Parigot Père & Fils (Meloisey) Range of excellent wines: Bourgogne Aligoté, Meursault les Vireuilles-Dessous, red Hautes-Côtes de Beaune, Beaune Grèves and Pommard.

PLACES OF INTEREST

In various villages of Hautes-Côtes de Beaune and in St-Romain there are well signed walking routes.

The Côte Chalonnaise

Just south of Santenay the Côte d'Or comes to an end, but Burgundy by no means finishes here. Continue on to the next belt of vines, the Côte Chalonnaise, which takes its name from the town of Chalon to the east. Its northern anchor-point is the lovely town of Chagny.

Even though the Côte Chalonnaise is a direct continuation of the Côte d'Or, the landscape is entirely different. Vineyards mingle here with many other crops, there are fields filled with goats and white Charolais cattle, and woods. Vineyards are found throughout this charming leafy and sleepy region.

The wines from the Chalonnais are less famous than those of the Côte d'Or. This is because most of the wine produced in this district has historically been sold as straight Bourgogne without any other regional reference. But the Chalonnais now has five appellations of its own. Four of these are connected to communes or groups of communes. They are, from north to south, Bouzeron, Rully, Mercurey (by far the largest), Givry and Montagny.

A good place to start discovering Chalonnaise wines is the Maison des Vins de la Côte Chalonnaise in the city of Chalon-sur-Saône. Although Chalon is not actually within the wine district, the Maison des Vins holds wines from all over the region and you can both taste and buy wine here. The best white wines from the region are made with Chardonnay and the reds with Pinot Noir, although the Aligoté thrives well on this terrain and much of it is used to make Bourgogne Côte Chalonnaise. This appellation was created as recently as 1989 and can be used on the labels of red and white burgundies from the 44 specified communes dotted around the main villages, if they attain the high quality standards demanded by the tasting panel. The quality of Bourgogne Côte Chalonnaise is such that it is rapidly gaining a good reputation.

Winemakers in the Chalonnais, particularly around the village of Rully, also produce some excellent Crémants de Bourgogne, as well as Bourgogne Passe-Tout-Grains – a red wine made from a mixture of Pinot Noir and Gamay.

Left *These vines in Montagny, at the southernmost end of the Côte Chalonnaise, produce white wines of good body and refreshing acidity.*

Above *A country lane running alongside vineyards. Beautiful rural sights like this become more frequent as you travel further south.*

NORTHERN CHALONNAIS

Leaving Santenay and travelling in an easterly direction you will reach the largest city in northern Chalonnais – Chagny. This is really an industrial town and so much so that only once a year is the emphasis on wine. That is during the wine exchange which takes place in the middle of August.

Chagny does, however, have some attractive old buildings well worth visiting in the centre of the town. These include, on the corner of the Rue de la République and Rue de la Boutière, a stunning large house dating from the Middle Ages. Additionally, behind the town hall there is a peaceful garden with old wells and some ruins, while in a chapel of the sober Cistercian church, a copy of the cave of Lourdes has been made.

Below *This old house surrounded by colourful plants is typical of the region's sleepy, timeless character.*

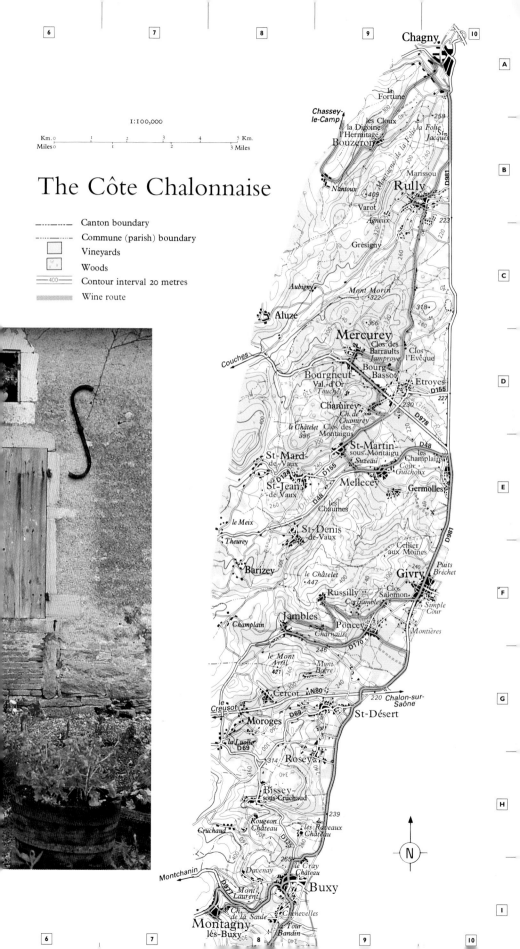

The Côte Chalonnaise

1:100,000

Km. 0   1   2   3   4   5 Km.
Miles 0   1   2   3 Miles

- ----·---- Canton boundary
- -----·----- Commune (parish) boundary
- Vineyards
- Woods
- 400 Contour interval 20 metres
- Wine route

BOUZERON

HOTELS

Auberge du Camp Romain
Chassey-le-Camp
Tel: 85 87 09 91
Peaceful hotel with views across the valley. Simply, but comfortably furnished. The restaurant cuisine is rather traditional (starting at about FF125 for a menu). Rooms start at approximately FF300. Swimming pool.

Hostellerie du Château de Bellecroix
Chagny
Tel: 85 87 13 86
Luxurious accommodation in an ivy bedecked castle. Rooms start at about FF550 – try to book one in one of the towers. Excellent restaurant with menus starting at around FF200. Swimming pool.

RESTAURANTS

Lameloise
Chagny
Tel: 85 87 08 85
Michelin-starred restaurant where the cooking is fantastic, the wine sublime. Menus start at FF400. Also a hotel.

Relais Gaulois
Nantoux
Tel: 85 87 33 00
Country inn on a hill. Regional dishes with menus starting at under FF100.

RECOMMENDED PRODUCERS

Chanzy Frères Domaine de l'Hermitage (Bouzeron)
This estate, founded in 1974, is among the best in Chalonnais. The whites (Bourgogne Aligoté, Bouzeron and Bourgogne Blanc especially) from the Clos de la Fortune are admirable.

A et P de Villaine (Bouzeron)
Aubert de Villaine is co-owner of the Domaine de la Romanée-Conti in Vosne-Romanée, but he also runs this well-respected property in Bouzeron with his wife Pamela. It produces exquisite wines, including the local Aligoté and an impressive white burgundy called Les Clous.

RELATED TO WINE

By taking, slightly to the south of Aluze, the D978 west, you reach the Couchois, a group of wine communes producing red and white burgundy as well as other generic wines. Included among these villages are Couches, Dracy-lès-Couches and St-Maurice-lès-Couches. The first two villages have impressive castles.

Above and right *Images of Rully – a sprawling village which produces equal quantities of red and white wine. The wines can offer good value for money and are often of a reasonable quality.*

Left *A large proportion of Crémant de Bourgogne is produced in Rully, although the base wine generally comes from other wine communes in the region.*

BOUZERON

From Chagny the narrow D219 runs southwest to the hamlet of Bouzeron. This is the home of a superior Bourgogne Aligoté, of such good quality that, since 1979, it has been allowed to be sold with the name of the village on the label.

For a touch of archeology and some marvellous views, take the winding road over the hill-tops to Chassey-le-Camp, via Nantoux. You see the village long before you reach it as it sits low down in the valley. On the west side are the remains of a large Neolithic settlement (3200–2000 BC) which were discovered in the 18th century. The spot can be reached on foot from the village and, although the long walk does not offer many archeological surprises, there is a marvellous panorama to be seen.

RULLY

From Bouzeron, return to the D981 and head south. All along the right side of the road are the Rully vineyards. A signpost indicates the right turn into the village.

The oldest part of the village stands on a hill, with most of the houses at its foot. This is because after the plague of 1347 the inhabitants fled the old village and built a new community on lower ground. There are a number of stately mansions, and the atmospheric triangular Place Sainte-Marie has a park where you can sit and relax.

From the centre of Rully, it is only a short stroll up the hillside to the west to Agneux where there are some interesting caves. The route is clearly shown by signposts.

The most important local building is Château de Rully, splendidly preserved on top of a hill and dominating the surrounding landscape. It has a square tower which dates from the 13th century. In front is a vineyard and behind it an English-style park which can be visited at weekends.

Winegrowing around Rully has revived since the 1970s, and in general the white wines – which are aromatic, fresh

RULLY

RESTAURANT

Le Vendangerot
Tel: 85 87 20 09
Situated on the Place Ste-Marie, this has a rather chic and at the same time rustic dining room. There is always a choice of various menus with regional dishes traditionally prepared. The most inexpensive menu costs less than FF100. It is also a simple hotel with large rooms from about FF200.

RECOMMENDED PRODUCERS

Jean-Claude Brelière
Passionate winegrower who produces a fresh, pure white Rully and a constantly improving red. A former language student, Brelière welcomes visitors from England, the US, Spain and Germany in their own tongue.

Michel Briday
A typically Burgundian atmosphere of disorderly scruffiness reigns here but, with careful searching, there are some delicious white wines.

André Delorme
The elongated cellar complex of this dynamic business is situated behind the local church. The main wine is sparkling, under the estate's own label as well as for a number of growers who do not have the know-how and equipment to make their own Crémant de Bourgogne. Délorme's own sparkling wine is excellent. The same family runs the large Domaine de la Renarde, whose wines include a first-class Rully and an equally attractive, minerally Montagny.

Domaine de la Folie
Between Chagny and Rully there is a hill on which the family Bouton has created the 'estate of foolishness'. The drive up to the house has a Provençal feel, being surrounded by pine and oak trees. The wines – mainly white and red Rullys – can be good.

Mercurey (right) has produced wine for centuries (see label far right). One of its most famous fans was Gabrielle d'Estrées, although her lover, Henri IV, preferred Givry.

Raymond Dureuil-Janthial
A reliable estate producing full-bodied white wines and firm reds.

Henri et Paul Jacqueson
A spotless winery, run with skill and passion and producing successful red wines from Rully and Mercurey. The white wine can also be good.

Domaine du Prieuré
This property belongs to a former Parisian restaurateur, Armand Monassier. It has a good reputation for its fruity white Rullys, its firm reds and the Crémant de Bourgogne.

Château de Rully
The Antonin Rodet firm has recently been working to turn this estate into one of the best and most highly valued in the appellation. Here you can enjoy fine wines, both white and red Rully, the latter characterized by wood and vanilla.

MERCUREY

RESTAURANT

Hostellerie du Val d'Or
Tel: 85 45 13 70
A large inn offering 13 spacious and comfortable rooms. In the rustic dining room you can enjoy tasty dishes based on regional ingredients (*le feuilleté de grenouilles aux champignons*), while inventive creations are also offered in '*Ma cuisine du moment*'. There is an impressive wine list. Menus start at about FF150 (weekdays). It is essential to ask for a room at the rear because the traffic at the front of the hotel is noisy.

RECOMMENDED PRODUCERS

Domaine Bordeaux-Montrieux
Supple, juicy red Mercureys. The owner is the director of the Domaine Thénard in Givry.

Luc Brintet et Frédéric Charles
Average-sized estate which produces pleasant-tasting Mercureys. The best ripen in new casks.

and fruity – have more depth than the reds and are usually excellent value for money. There are also a number of sparkling wine producers here; their Crémant de Bourgogne appellation is worth looking out for as these are often the richest *crémants* in Burgundy. Most of the still base wines used for Crémant de Bourgogne in Rully do not come from the local vineyards but from other Chalonnais communes.

MERCUREY

Leaving Rully heading south, you travel up, over and down a small hill, before turning right into the village of Mercurey.

This is the best-known village in the Chalonnais, where 95 percent of the vintage consists of red wine. That it has, thanks to wine, known periods of prosperity is shown by the large winegrowers' houses, most of which were built in the 18th and 19th centuries. In fact a number of Côte d'Or firms and estates have considerable holdings here and in the surrounding hamlets, including Philippe-le-Hardi (Santenay), Faiveley (Nuits-Saint-Georges) and Bouchard Aîné (Beaune). The Maison du Mercurey of the collective wine producers is

Michel Juillot

This is one of the largest, local, private estates, with arched cellars under an 18th-century building on the main street. The red wines taste rather firm and supple, while the white is sometimes worth a try.

Jean Maréchal

It is a pleasure to buy here – you can park easily opposite the cellar and the tasting is directed by Monsieur Maréchal who calmly talks about his wines' best points, passing quickly over any shortcomings, but always a pleasure to listen to. Many of his wines need patient cellaring, although some may be enjoyed when young and the prices are very reasonable.

Domaine de la Monette

Sturdy red Mercurey.

Antonin Rodet

A company in which the champagne firm Laurent Perrier has a controlling interest. The quality of the burgundies rose steadily in the 1980s. From its own land come the red and white Mercurey from Château de Chamirey (a hamlet near Mercurey).

PLACES OF INTEREST

By driving from Mercurey to Givry, you pass Germolles, on the south side of which is an interesting castle whose oldest part dates from the 12th century. It was formerly owned by Philip the Bold and can be visited.

located in Château de Garnerot, while Château de Chamirey (in the hamlet of the same name) is the property of Antonin Rodet, along with the wine tavern.

Mercurey has well over 2,000 inhabitants and consists mainly of one long street, which is dominated by striking copper lanterns. A side street, near Hostellerie du Val d'Or, runs upwards to Mercurey-le-Haut, where there is an 11th-century Romanesque church. On the other side of Mercurey stands the attractive church of Touches. It was built between the 12th and 15th centuries and has a monumental clock tower positioned in the middle of the nave. From Touches there is a lovely view of Mercurey.

Mercurey's red wines are usually sturdy and tasty, with concentrated fruit and firm tannin, if lacking in finesse. They have good potential for ageing rather than youthful charm. White Mercurey nowadays has more freshness and character than previously.

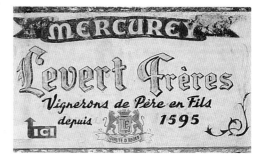

MERCUREY

Levert Frères

Vignerons de Père en Fils

depuis 1595

ICI

QUALITÉ D'ABORD

GIVRY

HOTEL

Le Dracy
Dracy-le-Fort
Tel: 85 87 81 81
This modern operation is situated next to a large orthopaedic centre. It has about 40 comfortable rooms (prices from about FF300). There is also a restaurant, La Garenne, where you can eat decently with menus from about FF100.

GIVRY

From Mercurey, you have a choice of routes to Givry, the third of the Chalonnais appellations. The long, more scenic, route takes you out of Mercurey heading east on the D978. After about one and a half kilometres, you turn right, into the village of Chamirey. At the crossroads in the centre of this hamlet, turn left and then hard right onto the D155 heading south towards Saint-Jean de Vaux. This route takes you through the hamlets of St-Martin-sous-Montaigu, Saint-Jean de Vaux, Saint-Denis de Vaux and Jambles. At Jambles, you turn left onto the D170 heading east and then northeast, passing through Poncey and entering Givry from the south. You will have travelled about 15 kilometres.

The shorter, more direct route from Mercurey to Givry is only seven kilometres. Leaving Mercurey the same way, heading east on the D978, you continue on this road until the T-junction where it joins the D981. You turn right onto this road, passing by the hamlet of Germolles on the right on your way to Givry, entering Givry from the north.

It has been said that Henry IV's mistress Gabrielle d'Estrées liked to drink Mercurey, but Henry himself preferred Givry, a story the winegrowers of Givry subscribe to and commemorate on many of their labels. Of all the wine communes in the Chalonnais, Givry is the richest in history, because its wine was already renowned in the 6th century and the Middle Ages. Around 1780 the village functioned as the wine centre for the entire region, and the enormous cellars of present day Domaine Thénard bear witness to this.

Nowadays, there is not much of this illustrious past to be seen. This does not mean that Givry is not worth a visit as the village does have some striking buildings. These include the Halle Ronde, along the main street, a round building with a spiral staircase (1830). Nearby is the town hall, which was completed in 1771 and built around a gateway, the Porte de l'Horloge with its small clock tower. Passing through the gateway, you come to a large, rectangular square which is dominated on the north side by a post office which looks more like a castle, with angels and grapes decorating a carved façade. From a distance you can see the large, octagonal church (designed by Emile Gauthey, who also designed the town hall) which is crowned by domes. The village is also dotted with several attractive fountains.

Like Mercurey, the district of Givry produces mainly red wines. These are strong, rounded, richly fruity and supple, with cherry-like aromas. The white wines are fresh, but at the same time firm and can be deliciously aromatic.

RESTAURANTS

Auberge de la Billebaude
Tel: 85 44 34 25
This bistro, near the church, offers regional and mainstream dishes at low prices. Usually also a fish menu and you can order *fondue vigneronne*.

Hôtel de la Halle
Tel: 85 44 32 45
Typical country restaurant, where the cooking is unpretentious, but tasty (*rôtis, grillades, lapin aux deux moutardes*, etc). The menus begin under FF100. It is also a simple hotel.

RECOMMENDED PRODUCERS

René Bourgeon (Jambles)
Active, small winegrower whose wines have received international awards.

Domaine Chofflet-Valdenaire (Russilly)
The Chofflet family has made wine here since 1710. The red Givry is very reliable as is the white.

Propriété Desvignes (Poncey)
Average-sized estate, of which the white Givry is quite aromatic and the red Givry Clos du Vernoy has sufficient power and backbone to benefit from some bottle-age.

Lumpp Frères
Exemplary Givrys.

Left *Grand architecture and vines in Givry.*
Below *Jambon persillé is perfect with Givry, due to the wine's delightful elegance and vibrant cherry (almost cranberry) fruitiness.*

Domaine Ragot (Poncey)
The white Givry here is generally more interesting than the red. Small, arched tasting cellar.

Clos Salomon
This estate, which goes back to the 14th century, produces only one wine, red Givry. It has a good colour, reasonable tannin and a pleasant dose of fruit.

Domaine Thénard
The family has owned its Givrys since 1760. The wines ferment and mature here in the magnificent 18th-century cellars. The estate also has land in the Côte d'Or and offers a high-quality range of wines including Le Montrachet, Grands Echézeaux, Corton Clos du Roi as well as the Givrys.

CHALON-SUR-SAONE

HOTELS

St-Georges
71100 Chalon-sur-Saône
Tel: 85 48 27 05
Comfortable hotel with a Michelin-starred restaurant. Rooms start at around FF400 and the menus range from FF150 to FF390.

CHALON-SUR-SAONE

From Givry it is only about five kilometres to Chalon-sur-Saône, the town from which the Chalonnais receives its name. Take the D981 heading south out of Givry and turn onto the N80 heading east to Chalon-sur-Saône.

With approximately 55,000 inhabitants, this city is the second largest in Burgundy, after Dijon and before Mâcon. Because of its location along the Saône River, it has been a centre for trade as far back as recorded history takes us. Its annual fairs were known throughout the whole of Europe. This is still the case for the Foire aux Sauvagines, a game market which takes place at the end of February.

The suburbs of Chalon are uninteresting, but the old centre has unquestionable charm. It fans out from behind the river quay and has many half-timbered houses. Along the quay itself there is, on a small square, the statue of Chalon's most famous son: Nicéphore Niépce (1765–1833) who made history by inventing photography. Near the statue is the Musée Niépce, which is one of the most important photographic museums in the world, exhibiting the history of photography in a fascinating and well laid-out way. The collection includes Niépce's equipment (and that of his pupil Daguerre, who was able to shorten the lighting process) and the world's very first photographs. There is also a design for a jet engine, another invention of Niépce, as well as an exhibition of modern equipment and contemporary photographs.

Above *Display of fresh vegetables in the local market.*
Right *Chalon, only five kilometres from Givry, is a charming and historical town, makes an ideal detour.*

From the museum, you can walk into the centre of the town and the town hall square (Place de l'Hôtel de Ville). Here you will find the church of Saint-Pierre, a Gothic-style building which was completed in the 18th century. Also on the square is the Musée Denon, which was founded in 1819 in a former monastery. It has many exhibits from prehistoric times, including finds from the excavation near Chassey-le-Camp, (see Northern Chalonnais, page 92). There are also finds from the Middle Ages and later periods. Besides paintings, the collection also contains marvellous pieces of furniture, nautical instruments and Egyptian art. The founder of the museum, Dominique Denon (1747–1825), took part in Napoleon's Egyptian campaign and became a celebrated Egyptologist.

Between the Place de l'Hôtel de Ville and the Place Saint-Vincent there is an attractive shopping street which runs parallel to the quay. The Place Saint-Vincent is surrounded by half-timbered houses, one of which is the 15th-century Maison aux Trois Greniers with its stunning balustrades. The church of Saint-Vincent, built and rebuilt between the 12th and 19th centuries, displays a multitude of sometimes unharmonious architectural styles but is still worth visiting. To one side is a three-galleried cloister.

From here it is a short walk to the Promenade Sainte-Marie where you will find the chalet-like Maison des Vins de la Côte Chalonnaise. This is a promotion centre for wines from the Chalonnais. Wines of every appellation,

Above *The cloisters of the Eglise St Vincent, in Chalon, built and rebuilt between the 12th and 19th centuries.*

St-Régis
71100 Chalon-sur-Saône
Tel: 85 46 22 81
Centrally located, well equipped hotel which also has a restaurant. Prices for rooms start around FF400. Restaurant closed Sundays. Menus start at FF98.

St-Jean
71000 Chalon-sur-Saône
Tel: 85 48 45 65
This reasonably priced hotel overlooks the river and has fairly simply furnished rooms from around FF230.

RESTAURANTS

Le Bourgogne
71100 Chalon-sur-Saône
Tel: 85 48 89 18
Beautifully situated in a 17th-century house. Menus start at about FF90. The restaurant is closed July 20 to 28.

L'Isle Bleue
71100 Chalon-sur-Saône
Tel: 85 48 39 83
Reasonably priced seafood restaurant. Menus start at around FF80. Closed from August 2 to 22.

Le Bistrot
71100 Chalon-sur-Saône
Tel: 85 93 22 01
Situated not far from the river, this good-value restaurant has menus from around FF85. Closed for August and on Saturday lunch-times and Sundays.

Right *View of Givry, with vines in foreground.*
Below *A wall painting in Buxy, location of one of Burgundy's largest and most influential cooperatives.*

MONTAGNY

HOTELS

Château Sassangy
Sassangy
Tel: 85 96 12 40
This 18th-century castle, which has recently been entirely renovated, has six rooms available following the *chambre d'hôte* formula (bed and breakfast). Traquility, stylish comfort and hospitality are the key words here. Prices start at about FF450 and you can also have dinner here. Sassagny is a few kilometres to the west of Buxy.

Le Relais du Montagny
Buxy
Tel: 85 92 19 90
This hotel, opened in 1990, is situated close to the local cooperative. Its 30 rooms are neat and functionally furnished, if a little on the small side. There is a swimming pool. It is owned by the proprietors of Girardot restaurant.

RESTAURANT

Girardot
Buxy
Tel: 85 92 04 04
Regional dishes (*poulet de Bresse aux morilles*) are offered in a simple ambience. Menus start at about FF100. When the weather is fine you can eat outside.

selected by a jury of local experts, can be bought here. You may also taste the wines and there is a simple restaurant, La Feuillette, where regional and grilled dishes are served at reasonable prices.

Otherwise, simply wander along the river. Groups of men play the implicitly French *jeu de boules* near here and there is a bridge which crosses the river to the Ile Saint-Laurent. On the west side of this small island, next to an enormous lime tree, is the hexagonal Tour du Doyenné. It is sometimes open to visitors and if you are feeling energetic you can climb to the top and admire the beautiful view of the city. This tower formerly stood next to the church of Saint-Vincent but, in 1926, with the help of a rich American, it was moved stone by stone to its present location.

Golf-lovers can also enjoy themselves in Chalon-sur-Saône, because on the east bank, in a loop of the river, the city has set out a fine, 18-hole golf course.

MONTAGNY

To reach Montagny from Chalon, retrace the route back along the N80 in a westerly direction. Look out for the turn off onto the D981 and take the southbound route for Buxy and Montagny. If you go north on the D981 you will end up back in Givry.

The D981 follows the contour of the hills into the village of Buxy. That the wines of Montagny, the southernmost district of the Chalonnais, were formerly sold as Côte de Buxy is completely understandable, because apart from Montagny-lès-Buxy and Buxy, the nearby villages of Jully-lès-Buxy and Saint-Vallerin also fall within the Montagny appellation. Buxy is by far the largest commune of the four. In the 12th century the village was fortified, two towers being the only remaining evidence of this. Near the Tour Rouge there is a large, humourous wall painting, depicting, with tongue in cheek, the wines from the surroundings. Some of the surrounding houses, or parts of them, date back as far as the Middle Ages. The only wine cooperative of the district is also found in Buxy.

Just as the name suggests, Montagny-lès-Buxy is largely situated on a hill. The streets are narrow and the vineyards run from the village centre downwards into a broad U-shaped valley. Jully-lès-Buxy, just like Montagny, offers a panoramic view over the area, while Saint-Vallerin has a Romanesque church. Slightly to the south of this wine village is the hamlet of La Tour, where the remains of an enormous medieval building can be seen.

The wines of Montagny are exclusively white made from the Chardonnay grape and are characterized by sturdy, juicy flavours with a light nuttiness. Although they may lack the liveliness and individuality of white Rullys, these wines can offer some of the best value for money for white wines in the whole of Burgundy. It used to be the case that all Montagny of 11.5 percent or stronger could be sold as Premier Cru, regardless of the vineyard site. That curious rule has now been reversed and the best vineyards have been formally identified as Premiers Crus – all 53 of them. The best-known are Montcuchot and Les Coères.

RECOMMENDED PRODUCERS

Pierre Bernollin (Jully-lès-Buxy)
Good Montagny wines here as well as Crémant de Bourgogne.

Cave des Vignerons de Buxy (Buxy)
Behind the old business premises of this cooperative is a modern cellar complex which is one of Burgundy's showpieces, where new equipment is invented and tested – many New World winemakers have visited here to see the complex. The red Bourgogne Pinot Noir is well worth tasting, as is the Montagny.

Bernard Michel (St-Vallerin)
Small producer of, among others, Montagny Les Coères.

Château de la Saule
This castle is situated at the foot of the village of Montagny and is the property of Alain Roy-Thévenin. His Montagny (ordinary and Premier Cru) is delicious and one of the most beautiful of the entire appellation.

Veuve Steinmaier & Fils (Montagny)
Various types of Montagny, the best being the buttery Montcuchot.

Jean Vachet (St-Vallerin)
Since 1959 this serious winegrower has extended his estate bit by bit and now produces some excellent wines. One of the best is the pure, generous Montagny Les Coères.

Below The charming village of Jully-lès-Buxy, like many in Burgundy, is situated on a hill overlooking its vines.

The Mâconnais

Retrace the route back into Buxy in order to rejoin the D981 heading south. Travelling along this road you will cross an imperceptible boundary between the Côte Chalonnaise and the Mâconnais. When you see signposts for the village of Saint-Gengoux-le-National you know you have arrived in the Mâconnais.

Although there are no clearly defined signs that you have passed from one wine region to another, there are some clues. The landscape remains agricultural, with crops other than grapes being grown and lush meadows on which Charolais cattle graze. As you continue south, a small ridge rises up followed by broad hills with wooded tops. Then come the first hints of the Mediterranean south – houses with Provençal red-tiled roofs and open-galleried façades.

Even more than the Chalonnais, the Mâconnais is a district of peaceful villages, whose silhouettes are often determined by a Romanesque church. Romanesque architecture in Burgundy probably first flowered in Cluny, where the Benedictine monks had their headquarters. The region is named after the city of Mâcon situated on the River Saône. There is strong historical evidence that the Romans made wine here, but it was the monks at Cluny in the 11th and 12th centuries who really made viticulture flourish. The wines they made enjoyed local fame but it was not until the 17th century that they found wider recognition. The story has it that a local grower, Claude Brosse, loaded two casks of his wine onto a cart and travelled for 33 days, braving bad roads and highwaymen, until he arrived at the court of Versailles. King Louis XIV is said to have been very impressed by the man and his wine, declaring it to be of a better quality than the Loire wines he had been drinking. And so Mâcon wines made their name.

Left *Cluny demands a visit, not just for its beauty, but for its place in the history of the wines of Burgundy.*

Above *The impressive Solutré rock dominates its surrounding landscape.*

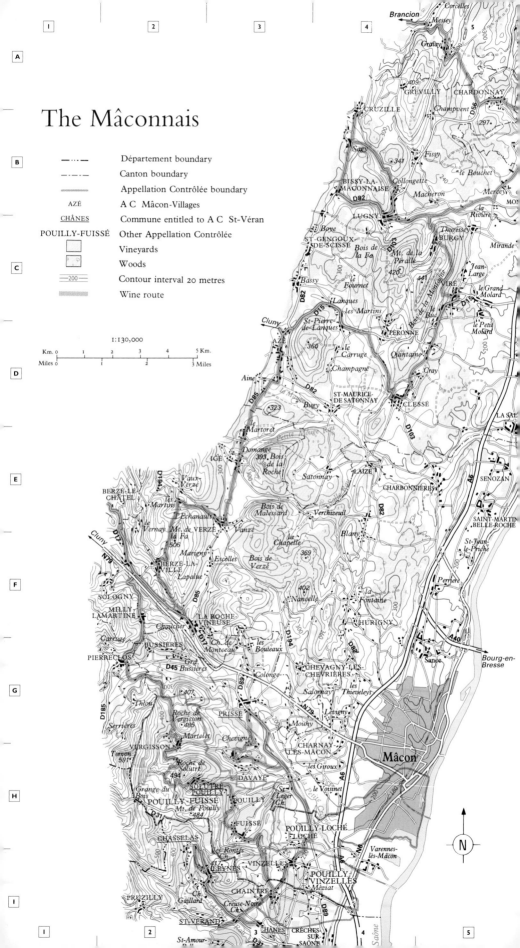

The Mâconnais

—··—··—	Département boundary
—·—·—	Canton boundary
———	Appellation Contrôlée boundary
AZÉ	A C Mâcon-Villages
CHÂNES	Commune entitled to A C St-Véran
POUILLY-FUISSÉ	Other Appellation Contrôlée
▢	Vineyards
▢	Woods
—200—	Contour interval 20 metres
▦	Wine route

1:130,000

Km. 0   1   2   3   4   5 Km.
Miles 0   1   2   3 Miles

The weather here already begins to take on a Mediterranean character, which means that the grapes ripen a little earlier than in the rest of Burgundy and the harvest is usually a week or two earlier. About 90 percent of the region's wine comes from cooperatives and, while in the past it has been the reds which have dominated, it is now the white wines which are more important, in terms of both quantity and quality, with Chardonnay grapes grown in roughly two-thirds of the vineyards.

The biggest appellation is Mâcon-Villages, or Mâcon followed by a village name. Other white wines can be labelled as Mâcon and Mâcon Supérieur (1 percent more alcohol). These last two are also appellations for red wines, with most labelled under the Supérieur category. The grape used for red wines in the region is the Gamay, and some Pinot Noir is also grown and used in blends.

The best, most famous and most expensive wines are produced in the extreme south of the region and are exclusively white – Pouilly-Fuissé, Pouilly-Vinzelles, Pouilly-Loché and Saint-Véran.

NORTHERN MACONNAIS

The mountain chain of the Mâconnais runs parallel with the A6 Autoroute du Soleil from the town of Tournus in the north of the region to Mâcon further south. The city of Mâcon lies just a few kilometres outside the appellation to the east. The northern Mâconnais is one of the most delightful parts of Burgundy to explore, as the beautiful countryside offers many wonderful views from the hilltops over the surrounding hills and valleys, and it also produces some excellent (mainly white) wines.

Below *A row of houses in the medieval hamlet of Brançion.*

Right *The immense, lavish interior decoration on the walls and ceiling of the Château de Cormatin.*

Below *View of the château at Brançion seen through an old stone archway.*

NORTHERN MACONNAIS

HOTELS

Auberge du Château
Tel: 85 33 28 02 (Cruzille)
A simple hotel (six rooms starting at about FF150) with a restaurant where you can eat for under FF100. Open from Easter through October.

Auberge du Vieux Brançion
Tel: 85 51 03 83 (Briançon)
Near the castle. Six simple rooms (two with bath or shower) starting at about FF170. The restaurant serves inexpensive regional dishes.

Hôtel du Centre
Tel: 85 33 22 82 (Lugny)
Village hotel with ordinary and smart rooms (10 rooms, starting at about FF170), a bar and a restaurant: tasty dishes using local ingredients and excellent wines from the local cooperative. Reasonable prices. Friendly service.

Château de Fleurville
Tel: 85 33 12 17 (Fleurville)
Castle hotel with park, not far from the *route nationale*. 15 rooms (starting at around FF430); good restaurant (menus from about FF165). Swimming pool.

The following touring route takes in all the major Mâconnais wine villages, as well as following some of the most picturesque roads through the region. From Buxy in the Chalonnais, follow the D981 travelling south towards the village of Cormatin. This village marks the beginning of the tour of the northern Mâconnais.

Before you start the tour proper, you might like to take the opportunity of stopping in Cormatin to visit the 17th-century castle there with its six charmingly furnished rooms. To start the wine tour, leave Cormatin driving in an easterly direction on the D14 to Brançion, a medieval hamlet situated on a steep slope beside a fortress which was once one of the most important fortifications of southern Burgundy. The village – cars are forbidden – has 14th-century market halls as well as a Romanesque church with some amazing frescos. From Brançion, continue east on the D14 to Ozenay. Turn right here onto the D463 travelling south, then left onto the D163. At the next T-junction, turn left onto the D56 which then brings you into the village of Chardonnay.

Up to this point vineyards have scarcely been seen. This changes near Chardonnay. No-one is absolutely certain, but it is thought that this ancient hamlet may possibly have given its name to the famous white grape variety.

Château d'Igé
Tel: 85 33 33 99 (Igé)
Luxurious accommodation with 13
spacious, finely furnished rooms and
apartments (starting at around
FF500). The cuisine is high quality
with a classic touch. Menus start at
about FF200.

Le Montagne de Brançion
Tel: 85 51 12 40 (Brançion)
High up on a hill in the vicinity of
Brançion. Beautiful view from all 20
rooms (starting at about FF400).
They have been furnished with taste
and offer adequate comfort. Good
restaurant. Outdoor swimming pool.

Relais Lamartine
Tel: 85 36 64 71 (Bussières)
Peacefully situated hotel with eight
rooms (starting at about FF360). You
can eat breakfast and lunch outside
when the weather permits. Menus
start at about FF100. A speciality is
*parfait de foies de volaille aux baies
de cassis.*

RESTAURANTS

Le Relais de Mâconnais
Tel: 85 36 60 72 (La Croix Blanche)
The superb cuisine attracts many
guests with menus starting at about
FF140. Varied menu, with a regional
accent (*aiguillettes de filet de Charolais
au Mâcon rouge*). Also a hotel.

UCHIZY

The route continues east on the D163
to Uchizy, a wine village with a strikingly large church with frescoes and a
five-storey tower. Now take the D120
travelling southwest, through Mercey,
turning right onto the D103 shortly
afterwards and into Burgy with its
11th-century church and panoramic
view over the valley. The road continues southwards to Viré. At the higher
part of this village there is a church
with a pointed tower, and in the lower
area, you will find the wine cooperative, the Château des Cinq Tours (a
16th-century wine estate) and the village square with its statue of Bacchus.

Via Quintaine the route continues
south to Clessé where the stainless steel
tanks of the wine cooperative contrast
with the little 11th-century church and its octagonal tower.
At Clessé turn right heading west towards Saint-Maurice de
Satonnay on the D403b, turning left there to head south to
the village of Satonnay. At the T-junction after Satonnay,

Above *Enchanting tree-covered walk
in the gardens of the 17th-century
Château de Cormatin — there are also
delightfully furnished rooms to visit.*

Relais de Montmartre
Tel: 85 33 10 72 (Viré)
Well cared-for inn on village square.
Stylish interior, nice service, regional
cuisine. Menus begin under FF100.

St-Pierre
Tel: 85 33 20 27 (Lugny)
Simple restaurant. There is also a
wine-tasting room. Regional dishes
and local wines. Panoramic view.

SPECIAL INTEREST

Goat's cheese is served everywhere
in Mâconnais, in all possible variations.

RECOMMENDED PRODUCERS

**Auvigue-Burrier-Revel
(Charnay-lès-Mâcon)**
Small *négociant* firm, specializing in
white Mâconnais, especially St-Véran
and Pouilly-Fuissé. It sells the wines of
several estates, also buying in grapes
for vinification. The wines are the
opposite of big, open Chardonnays
from the New World. They are lean,
discreet and usually need cellaring.

turn right onto the D434 through the beautiful Bois de
Malessard and into Verzé from where you can enjoy a fabu-
lous panoramic view across southern Mâconnais. According
to legend the water from the village fountain here has healing powers. Partridges are bred for hunting at the 11th-
century Château d'Escolle.

From Verzé, take the road down the valley to La Roche
Vineuse, with its 12th-century bell-tower and views over the
Charolais countryside. In the hamlet
of Eau-Vive, just outside La Roche
Vineuse, there is an open-air museum,
Au Bout du Monde, with houses from
various cultures, including African.

From here turn right onto the
N79 and drive westward to Berzé-la-
Ville with its Romanesque church
and – just outside the village – La
Chapelle aux Moines. This 11th-
century chapel is famous for its rich,
Byzantine wall paintings. There is
also another beautiful view from a
point near the chapel.

From Berzé-la-Ville, take the road heading north to Le Cloux and then take the D194 which follows the contours of the Mont de Verzé, winding slowly round to the east and back to Verzé. From here take the D85 northwards to the village of Igé. On the north side of Igé stands the 11th-century chapel of Domange. During weekends and on holidays you can visit the Musée de la Vigne, including a wine-tasting room which is situated in the chapel. Continue north

on the D85 to Azé where, in the season, you can visit the prehistoric caves and archeological museum. The village also has a Romanesque church and an old market hall.

Travelling north from Azé, you pass through Saint-Gengoux-de Scisse and on to Bissy-la-Mâconnaise where, in the massive Romanesque church tower, there are interesting wooden statuettes of the saints. Then, driving east on the D82, you arrive in Lugny. On a hill above this village is the most important wine cooperative of the Mâconnais, with a tasting and sales room. On the south side of Lugny's main street is a large 16th-century church and two round towers which are all that remain of a 16th-century castle.

After Lugny, carry on along the D56 but take the left fork at Collongette, driving along the narrow valley floor (the road running parallel with a stream) until you

Domaine André Bonhomme (Viré) Well-respected winemaker who produces pure, tasty Mâcon-Viré usually matured in barrels for six months. He also keeps bees and you can buy honey as well as wine here.

Château des Cinq Tours (Viré) Beautiful Mâcon-Viré.

Collin et Bourisset (Crèches-sur-Saône) Nice table wines, particularly the two Moulin-à-Vents in the range.

Coopérative de Chardonnay (Chardonnay) Dominating winemaking in the village of Chardonnay, this cooperative has above-average quality expectations. One of the award-winning wines is the Mâcon-Chardonnay.

Domaine de Chervin (Burgy) Mainly white Mâcon and Mâcon-Burgy. Both charming, with a soft-fresh taste.

Coopérative Charnay-lès-Mâcon (Charnay-lès-Mâcon) St-Véran is the speciality, but the Mâcon-Villages has just as much class.

Cooperative Clessé (Clessé) The wine produced the most here is the juicy white Mâcon-Clessé, which is bottled by the cooperative itself.

Cooperative Igé Reliable wines. Above all white Château London (a Mâcon-Igé) and the ordinary Mâcon-Igé are worth tasting.

Cooperative Lugny (Lugny) This is the largest cooperative in Burgundy, producing four million bottles a year. The wines are good, especially the Crémant de Bourgogne, white Mâcon-Lugny Les Charmes, red Mâcon and Mâcon Supérieur and Bourgogne Passe-Tout-Grains.

Cooperative Mancey (Mancey) The white wines above all are worth tasting here, such as the white Mâcon (Supérieur) and Burgundy.

Cooperative Viré (Viré) Reliable white Mâcon-Viré. The Crémant de Bourgogne produced here is also tasty.

Domaine Goyard (Viré) Excellent white Mâcon-Viré.

Henri Lafarge (Bray) Pleasant wines: rather full, lightly nutty white Mâcon as well as red Mâcon-Bray and the basic Bourgogne.

Left Detail of the old stone clock-tower at Uchizy, one of 43 villages entitled to sell its wines under the name 'Mâcon' and its own name. Far left The château at Brançion – once one of the most important fortifications in southern Burgundy – and (above left) the landscape that surrounds it.

Domaine Manciat-Poncet (Lévigny)
Wines fermented in stainless steel (Mâcon-Charnay) and small oak casks (Pouilly-Fuissé). Both are excellent.
Domaine de Montbellet (Lugny)
Deliciously fresh white Mâcon-Villages, often with spicy hints.
Domaine de Roally (Viré)
Aromatic, complex Mâcon-Viré. Top quality but small production.
Domaine Talmard (Uchizy)
Successful large estate producing some excellent white wines, especially the Mâcon-Uchizy and Mâcon-Villages.
Jean Thévenet (Quintaine)
One of the outstanding domaines of the Maconnais. White Mâcon-Clessé of impeccable quality, usually with fruity aroma.
Trénel Fils (Charnay-lès-Mâcon)
The white as well as the red wines are rich in fruit. Especially fine are the Mâcon-Villages, St-Véran, Pouilly-Fuissé, Crus from Beaujolais and red Mâcon.

WINE FESTIVALS

During the second half of May, one of France's largest wine fairs takes place annually in Mâcon. And in Créches-sur-Saône, along the N6, the Cellier-Expo is situated, where information about the wine area and a wine route is given. Also during the Palm Sunday weekend Lugny has a wine fair.

reach the hamlet of Sagy. Turn right here and on into Cruzille. Just before this village, on the left side of the road, the Musée des Outils d'Autrefois exhibits about 3,500 tools from the past. Cruzille also has a well-preserved 14th-century castle, which now houses a medical institute.

CLUNY

No tour of the northern Mâconnais is complete without visiting the fascinating town of Cluny. The following route makes for a pretty and relaxed drive. You must retrace the route back to the village of Azé, turning right there onto the D15 to Cluny. This marvellous road runs past the charming village of Donzy-le-Pertuis (with its 11th-century church) and through the beautiful forests of Cluny.

Cluny itself is steeped in history. The Benedictine monastery founded there in the 10th century became the biggest and most powerful in Europe. The ruins of the abbey church, and the model of it in its heyday, do much to show how impressive the complex must have been.

From Cluny, drive south on the D980 to Berzé-le-Châtel. This hill village is dominated by a massive castle with 13 towers (12th to 15th century) which was once the seat of the first barony of the Mâconnais. Follow the same road south to the pretty, sleepy village of Milly-Lamartine, where the poet and politician Alphonse de Lamartine (see Mâcon page 114) spent his youth. A bust of the famous poet can be found here, as well as a charming Romanesque church. It is not far from here to Pierreclos with its 14th-century castle, which is now a museum, and, for those who enjoy walking, there is a Lamartine walking route around these last two villages. The village of Pierreclos also has some of the finest vineyards in the Mâcon appellation.

This completes the tour of the northern Mâconnais. From here the journey can be continued in a southerly direction to Vergisson and the district of Pouilly-Fuissé.

Above *A directional sign for the* Caveau Dégustation *by a roadside.*
Right *View of the landscape and chapel at Berzé le Châtel.*
Far right *The elegant interior of the Abbey of Cluny, a sight that should not be missed when visiting the area.*

MACON

HOTELS

Mercure-Altéa Mâcon
26 Rue Coubertin
Tel: 85 38 28 06
One of Mâcon's two best hotels.
Comfortable and well equiped
rooms (63) with pleasant views, from
about FF470. Also has a restaurant
Le St-Vincent, with menus from
about FF100.

Bellevue
416 Quai Lamartine
Tel: 85 38 05 07
Wonderful location overlooking the
river in the centre of Mâcon and
peaceful due to sound proofing.
Comfortable rooms (24) priced from
FF400. Also has a restaurant and
menus start at FF90.

Nord
313 Quai Jean Jaurès
Tel: 85 38 08 68
Medium-sized hotel located on the
River Saône. Fairly comfortable
rooms priced from about FF190.
Closed November to March.

Right *The entrance to a*
boulangerie-patisserie *in the*
fascinating old city of Mâcon.

Burgundy is full of shops selling
wonderful delicacies such as:
Above *Artichokes and endives.*
Top *A selection of luxurious*
patisserie.

MACON

Mâcon is situated, just like Chalon-sur-Saône, on the River
Saône, east of the main Mâconnais wine region. To reach it,
drive east on the N79. The town has about 40,000 inhabitants, and dates back to Roman times when it was an important garrison settlement full of workshops making spears and
arrows for both soldiers and hunters. Winegrowing was
already practised around Mâcon at that time; the poet
Ausonius mentions it in his writing.

Mâcon's places of interest are mainly found in the old
centre, along the Saône. The poet and politician Alphonse
de Lamartine (1790–1869) was born in Mâcon, and there
are constant reminders of this fact as you wander through
the town. A street, a quay and a promenade have been named
after him, and in the Hôtel Senecé (Rue Sigorne) a
museum has been devoted to him. What is more, you can see

a life-size Lamartine surrounded by other personages in an enormous mosaic on the side of a wall (corner of Rue Gambetta and Rue Edouard-Herriot).

On the quay, close to the statue of the famous citizen, is the Hôtel Montrevel, an imposing, pala-tial building from the 18th century which today is used as the town hall. Directly behind lies a lively shopping street and the strikingly designed Office du Tourisme. Here you can ask for entrance to the chapel of the Résidence Soufflot, previously a hos-pital, which is situated nearby. The chapel is built in an unusual oval form and in the small tower to the right of the gateway is a small hatch through which unwanted babies could be discretely handed over to the hos-pital in days gone by.

Across from the Office du Tourisme is the neo-Romanesque church of Saint-Pierre with its elegant, pointed towers. By following the shopping street in a northerly direction, you arrive at the Place aux Herbes, with the Maison de Bois on a corner. This is the oldest building of Mâcon – and is the city's most famous. On the wooden façade of the building are numerous small sculptures of peo-ple and animals in various unusual settings. After walking to the end of the shopping street you reach the Vieux Saint-Vincent. This was a cathedral which has been repeatedly destroyed over the centuries; all that remains now are two, unequal, octagonal towers. Continuing west you will find the Musée des Ursulines, which houses a col-lection of historic objects and works of art. The oldest date from the prehistoric age and were found near Solutré (see Pouilly-Fuissé page 116). The glass windows and ceramics are also interesting to see.

Concorde
73 Rue Lacretelle
Tel: 85 34 21 47
Small hotel situated on the other side of the town centre, away from the river. Fairly comfortable rooms starting at about FF190.

RESTAURANTS

Mâcon has a good and varied selection of restaurants. The finest, though, are situated in some of the neighbouring villages, such as Georges Blanc in Vonnas. The following are just a small selection:

Le Saint-Laurent
1 Quai Bouchacourt
Tel: 85 39 29 19
This bistro-style restaurant has wonderful views over the river and outside seating is available. Menus from around FF150.

Pierre
7 Rue Dufour
Tel: 85 38 14 23
Located in the old town, just behind the Bellevue hotel, this restaurant offers menus from around FF100.

L'Amandier
74 Rue Dufour
Tel: 85 39 82 00
Further along the same street as the Pierre, this restaurant is quite popular among local winegrowers. Menus from around FF100.

Le Poisson d'Or
Allée Parc (one kilometre along the Saône from the town centre)
Tel: 85 38 00 88
Beautifully located restaurant in a shaded spot on the river bank. Menus from about FF100.

Left *View of the riverside buildings overlooking the Saône River in the centre of Mâcon. See the listings for a selection of hotels and restaurants located nearby.*

POUILLY-FUISSE

HOTEL

La Vigne Blanche
Fuissé
Tel: 85 35 60 50
Simple rooms (starting at about
FF200). In the unpretentious
restaurant you can eat Burgundian
dishes such as frog's legs and *coq au
vin*; a few regional wines are served
by the glass. The menus begin under
FF100.

RESTAURANTS

Chez Cantal
Vergisson
Tel: 85 35 84 69
Simple establishment which serves
just one *plat du jour*. Small terrace,
across from the church.

Le Petit Trou
Vinzelles
Tel: 85 35 60 24
Café offering a cheap *menu du jour*.

Au Pouilly-Fuissé
Fuissé
Tel: 85 35 60 68
The best restaurant of the district. In
the light interior you can enjoy tasty,
regional dishes such as *mousseline de
brochet à la crème de cèpes, poulet rôti
à la fleur de thym* or *andouillette
braisée à la moutarde*. The weekday
menu is often less than FF100. The
ordinary menus begin at about FF115.

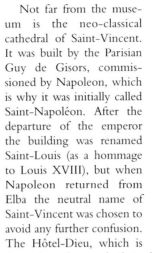

Not far from the museum is the neo-classical cathedral of Saint-Vincent. It was built by the Parisian Guy de Gisors, commissioned by Napoleon, which is why it was initially called Saint-Napoléon. After the departure of the emperor the building was renamed Saint-Louis (as a hommage to Louis XVIII), but when Napoleon returned from Elba the neutral name of Saint-Vincent was chosen to avoid any further confusion. The Hôtel-Dieu, which is situated nearby, was built in the 18th century and is dominated by a large, ellipse-shaped dome. On the ground floor there is a chemist where you can see a fine collection of pots from the time of Louis XV.

Slightly to the north of Mâcon's old centre, in an area of parkland, lies the Maison Mâconnaise des Vins (484 Avenue de Lattre-de-Tassigny). Here you can taste and buy wines from Mâconnais and northern Beaujolais, and enjoy a meal in the restaurant.

POULLY-FUISSE

There is no doubt that Pouilly-Fuissé is the most famous wine from the Mâconnais – and also the most expensive. The appellation lies directly to the west of the city of Mâcon and can be recognized from a distance by two steeply rising rocks, which seem to cut through a stormy sea of green grape-vines like the petrified bows of ships. These are the cliffs of Vergisson (to the north) and Solutré (to the south). From Mâcon, travel west on the N79 and, after about five or six kilometres, turn left onto the D45 to Pierreclos.

At Pierreclos (Mâcon and Mâcon-Villages appellations), turn left onto the D177, arriving in the village of Vergisson after about two kilometres. This is a small village with sloping streets and a steep cliff towering high above the pointed church spire. Parts of the cliff are ochre and pink in colour and a cave has been found nearby with the remains of a Neanderthal man. In the hamlet of Chancerons, on the south side of Vergisson, is a three-metre-high menhir.

From Vergisson there runs a narrow, winding road through wooded slopes to Solutré. The cliff above this

Above Sign on the side of a house
in Fuissé advertising one of the
town's many wine producers.
Above right A stage of the
cheese-making process, which can
sometimes be as lengthy and
painstaking as winemaking.

Left *The dramatic, towering presence of the Solutré rock above an expanse of vines. The majority of these grapes are used for the production of Pouilly-Fuissé.*

village is even more impressive than that of Vergisson. Legend has it that the Gallic leader Vercingetorix lit a fire on the rock in order to assemble the tribes before the struggle for independence. This is remembered on Saint-John's day (Midsummer's day) each year with a large bonfire on the same spot.

In 1866 the remains of a prehistoric hunting camp were found at the foot of the rock, including the fossilized bones of thousands of horses which are believed to have been driven off the top of the cliff to their death by hunters, between 35000 and 10000BC. Excavations have resulted in one of Europe's richest collections of prehistoric objects, some of which can be seen in the Musée Départemental de Préhistorie, in Solutré. Apart from hunting tools, the museum, which was opened in 1987, has statuettes, including a small sculpture of a mammoth.

Solutré itself is a charming village. In the Caveau Pouilly-Fuissé you can taste the local wine (for a fee) and buy bottles of it. Diagonally opposite stand the church (Romanesque, 12th-century) and La Boutique, a store for wine, wine-related articles, jewellery, ceramics and other items.

It is also a good place for walking – keen and energetic walkers can climb to the top of the Solutré cliff, where the

RECOMMENDED PRODUCERS

Château de Beauregard (Fuissé)
Important estate which produces distinguished wines, fermented in wooden casks.

Cave des Grands Crus Blancs (Vinzelles)
Cooperative dominating the district, accounting for about 80 per cent of the production of both Pouilly-Vinzelles and Pouilly-Loché.

Louis Curveux (Fuissé)
Excellent wines.

Château Fuissé (Fuissé)
For years this has been the appellation's prime standard-bearer. Superb Pouilly-Fuissé Vieilles Vignes. Other great quality wines worth tasting here are the St-Véran and Morgon Charmes.

Roger Duboeuf & Fils (Chaintré)
Roger is the elder brother of the more famous Georges Duboeuf. Visitors can taste delicious wines, including white Beaujolais and Pouilly-Fuissé, in the 16th-century tasting room.

Domaine Guffens-Heynen (Vergisson)
The friendly Belgian owner Jean-Marie Guffens makes a small number of high-quality wines: Pouilly-Fuissé and white and red Mâcon-Pierreclos.

ST VERAN

RESTAURANTS

Au Fin Bec
Leynes
Tel: 85 35 11 77
Appetizing aromas waft from
this restaurant where the owner is
the cook. The cuisine is regional. A
couple of different menus for less
than FF100.

Relais Beaujolais-Mâconnais
Leynes
Tel: 85 35 11 29
Simple, regional dishes and indeed
regional wines. The menus begin
under FF100.

Le Tire Bouchon
St-Vérand
Tel: 85 37 15 33
A winegrowing family owns this
restaurant, situated at the foot of the
village. *Coq au Beaujolais-Villages,
entrecôte charolaise* and similar dishes.
Menus start at less than FF100.

exertion is rewarded with a wonderful view. There is also a
walking route starting from the hamlet of La Grange du
Bois, situated on a hill just outside Solutré. The view is fab-
ulous and as a treat afterwards you can eat, mainly *grillades,* in
the rustic Auberge de la Grange du Bois (*Tel: 85 37 80 78*).

By driving from Solutré to Fuissé, you pass through the
hamlet of Pouilly. In the higher part of the village, from
where there is a fine view of the surrounding countryside,
there is a 15th-century chapel and a castle, flanked by towers.

About one kilometre down the road is Fuissé, from
which Pouilly-Fuissé takes the second part of its name. The
village sits in a natural 'amphitheatre', the slopes of which
spread out from it, planted with its now world-famous
grape-vines. The important role wine has played in Fuissé's
history is demonstrated by the allegorical depiction of the
struggle against phylloxera above the entrance to its church.

From Fuissé, take the winding D172 west and turn left
onto the D31. This road takes you through the village of
Leynes. At the crossroads about one kilometre outside
Leynes, turn left to the village of Chaintré. On a wall near

the church is a colourful wall painting and a large bottle with the names of winegrowers reminding one once more that this is a wine village.

While a good Pouilly-Fuissé is a rich white wine which gives impressions of fruit, flowers, nuts and also often of vanilla and oak, there are two other local wines which have a slightly lighter structure, but which cost much less. These are Pouilly-Vinzelles and Pouilly-Loché. Unfortunately both of them are hard to find.

The origin of Pouilly-Vinzelles is the village of Vinzelles. To reach it, continue north from Chaintré. Pouilly-Loché originates from the village of Loché, which is another kilometre further north. The local castle, the Château de Loché (13th to 18th century), has made its own wine since 1989, but the quality is variable. It can be visited, but by appointment only.

ST-VERAN

The appellation of Saint-Véran was created in 1971 out of land in eight communes dotted haphazardly around the district: Chânes, Chasselas, Davayé, Leynes, Prissé, Saint-Amour, Saint-Vérand and Solutré. Formerly these villages produced Mâcon-Villages or white Beaujolais. As a wine, the (always white) Saint-Véran is usually somewhat leaner and less rich than Pouilly-Fuissé. There are exceptions though: a superior Saint-Véran, more usually from the communes of Prissé or Davayé, can often offer better quality than an average Pouilly-Fuissé.

The northern-most municipality is Prissé, situated on the D89 travelling north from Loché. There are two castles in this village, Manoir de la Cerve and Château de Monceau, neither of which is open to the public. The poet Bauderon lived in the first and Lamartine in the second.

About two kilometres to the south of Prissé is the neighbouring village of Davayé where there is more to see including, on a hillside nearby, a Romanesque church and an old communal bath. There are also several castles and a well-known school for winegrowing.

To the south of Chaintré is the village of Saint-Vérand. The village was formerly called Saint-Véran-des-Vignes, but the name was changed to avoid confusion with Saint-Véran in Beaujolais. Dating from the Middle Ages, this attractive hill village has a carefully restored, small church with a beautiful fresco inside.

At the village of Leynes you will find one of the very few 16th-century churches in Burgundy. It is situated near the village square.

Finally, you will come to the village of Chasselas, which gave its name to both a table and a wine grape (though no longer cultivated in this part of France). It is worth stopping off to see the small Romanesque church in the centre of the village and the large, attractive castle on the outskirts.

RECOMMENDED PRODUCERS

Domaine de la Croix Senaillet (Davayé) The St-Véran here is usually fresh, firm and fruity. The red Mâcon is distinguished by its fruit too.

Henri-Lucius Grégoire (Davayé) Modest property with some good St-Vérans and a Crémant de Bourgogne.

Jean-Jacques Martin (Chânes) Some delicious wines are produced here, fermented in stainless steel. Try the white Burgundy, St-Véran and a sublime Pouilly-Vincelles.

Domaine des Pérelles (Chânes) This estate is run by André Larochette and produces, among others, a successful St-Véran.

Cooperative Prissé (Prissé) Modern, well- equipped business. Excellent white wines. Try the St-Véran, Mâcon-Villages and Bourgogne Aligoté.

Domaine des Pierres Rouges (Chasselas) This estate enjoys a good name mainly because of its quite generous, soft, fresh St-Véran.

Domaine des Valanges (Davayé) A delicious, well-balanced St-Véran is made here, full of flavour and aroma.

PLACES OF INTEREST

On a hill behind the old church of Davayé stands the angular building complex of the Lycée Viticole de Davayé. Young winegrowers are educated here. It makes wine from its own vineyards, including a St-Véran.

Far left (bottom) *The Solutré Rock, and surrounding hills.*
Top *A street sign advertises the Maconnais' most famous wine.*
Main picture and above *The charming village of Solutré.*

Beaujolais

With more than one half of the total vineyards under its appellation, Beaujolais is by far the largest of the five Burgundian districts. It is also one of the most beautiful. It is made up of a long sequence of granite hills, the spurs of a chain of wooded mountains that vary in height from 700–1,000 metres. These hills act as a shield against westerly winds so that the region enjoys a mild climate. Narrow, winding roads criss-cross the district, past green hills, through quiet valleys and idyllic villages. In a timeless, romantic way the Beaujolais symbolizes the best of the French countryside. With good reason Gabriel Chevallier chose Vaux-en-Beaujolais as the model for his novel Clochemerle, the comic story of rural life, which has been translated into many languages.

Wine grapes reign supreme here, in particular the Gamay, or, to give it its full title, the Gamay Noir à Jus Blanc, which thrives in the sandy, stony or schistous soils of the district. Helped by the climate, these soils give the wines a rounded quality and depth of flavour which is seldom achieved elsewhere with this grape variety. There is also a certain amount of white Beaujolais made, based on Chardonnay.

The best and most powerful wines of Beaujolais are the ten Crus. These come from villages or groups of villages in the northern part of the area. These are, from north to south, Saint-Amour (part of which actually lies within the Mâconnais), Juliénas, Chénas, Moulin-à-Vent, Fleurie, Chiroubles, Morgon, Régnié, Brouilly and Côte de Brouilly.

Ordinary Beaujolais is mainly grown in the southern part of the district, with the slightly better quality, fuller Beaujolais-Villages wines produced in and around 39 villages, most of which are situated in the north of the region.

But the world has come to know the Beaujolais, not through its best wines but through its simplest – Beaujolais

Left Beaujolais offers Burgundy's most beautiful landscape.

Above Traditional sign made from the end of a barrel.

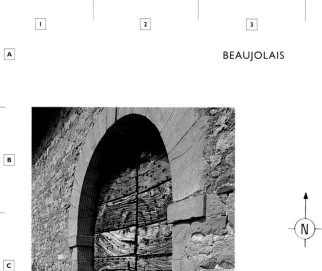

Above *The region of Beaujolais has remained relatively untouched by the passing of time, as this old wooden door illustrates.*

Beaujolais

—·—·—	Département boundary
—··—··—	Canton boundary
—···—···—	Commune (parish) boundary
⎯⎯⎯	Limits of Grands Crus
▢	Vineyards
⊕	Woods
—200—	Contour interval 20 metres
▨▨▨	Wine route

1:75,000

Km. 0   1   2   3 Km.

Miles 0   1   2 Miles

Primeur or Beaujolais Nouveau. This is sold from the third Thursday in November and is made to be drunk immediately. Commercially Beaujolais Nouveau has been a tremendous success with the result that it now represents about half of all Beaujolais production. But for true wine-lovers, finding really excellent examples of what can be achieved with the Gamay grape is the main aim and, if you look carefully, some are superb.

Fruit is characteristic of all good Beaujolais red wines, and the best offer juicy flavours of red fruits (strawberries, raspberries, cherries). They are often best served slightly chilled: about 16°C is ideal.

SAINT-AMOUR

The northernmost cru of Beaujolais, Saint-Amour, derives its name from the commune of Saint-Amour-Bellevue, which is made up of several hamlets. From Chânes in the southern Mâconnais, travel southeast, crossing over the D31 to join the D186.

The first hamlet you come to is the hill-top village of Le Bourg Neuf. From here the road (D186) runs through vineyards to Plâtre-Durand, a hamlet consisting mainly of a large square with two restaurants and a wine-tasting room, the Caveau du Cru Saint-Amour, which is open at weekends and holidays as well as during the week. A statue of a Roman legionary, near the reception hall of Saint-Amour-Bellevue, is witness to the legend that a soldier called Amor(e) or Amator, settled here at the end of the third century, having been converted to Catholicism, and was canonized because he was killed for his religion.

Further west along the same road is the hamlet of La Ville. On the hill above it is the Château de Saint-Amour, a 19th-century building built on the foundations of a 16th-century castle. Its wines are sold mainly through a *négociant*.

Saint-Amour wines are fairly reserved but have fruit, charm and supple structure. Like all the Crus, Saint-Amour wines must contain at least 10.5 percent alcohol, 11 percent if the name of the vineyard appears on the label.

JULIENAS

At Plâtre-Durand you must turn right onto the D486. After about three kilometres you arrive at the village of Juliénas.

The fact that this is a wine village is immediately clear to visitors who park their cars on the Place du Marché, because not only is there a shop selling wine cellar equipment (as well as wine-related items for the home), but there is also a shop owned by winegrower Pierre Perrachon (from Chénas) and a strikingly designed restaurant called Le Coq au Vin. Should there still be doubts then a walk in the direction of the church will dispel them, because across from the currently

ST-AMOUR

 RESTAURANT

Auberge du Paradis
Tel: 85 37 10 26
Village inn with menus under FF100.

RECOMMENDED PRODUCERS

Domaine de la Cave Lamartine
St-Amours full of fruit, including white.
Domaine des Ducs Family firm with
charming wines. St-Amour is award-
winning and among the very best.
André Poitevin Possibly the oldest
cellar in St-Amour, dating from 1399.
Intensely fruity and well-structured wines.
Domaine de Savy Excellent reds
and whites, eg St-Véran, Pouilly-Fuissé.
Georges Trichard Talented grower
with wines in top Paris restaurants.

JULIENAS

HOTEL

Hôtel des Vignes
Tel: 74 04 43 70
Peacefully situated with simple rooms.

RESTAURANT

Le Coq au Vin
Tel: 74 04 41 98
Stylish with excellent cuisine.

RECOMMENDED PRODUCERS

Domaine des Chers Juliénas with
fruit and potential to mature well.
Château de Juliénas Deserves a
visit to see its magnificent cellars.

Above *A chais in St-Amour.*
Above right *The commune of
Juliénas produces structured wines
which can age, although most should
be drunk after two to three years.*
Right *Local crafts on sale in
St-Amour.*
Far right *Domaine des Chers –
one of the best estates in Juliénas.*

used church is the old church – which, since 1954, has been
used as a wine-tasting room. The interior of this Cellier de
la Vieille Eglise is decorated with bacchanalian depictions
and attracts many visitors, especially at weekends.

The origins of this wine village apparently go back to
Roman times. Perhaps the name Juliénas is derived from
Julius Caesar – but this is also said to be the case for neigh-
bouring Jullié (whose vineyards belong to Juliénas too).

One of the oldest local buildings is the Château de
Juliénas, which is situated just outside the village centre on
the D137. It has impressive 18th-century cellars which cover
200 square metres. Slightly further along the same road is the
Maison de la Dîme, a tollhouse from the 16th century.
Juliénas also has an important wine cooperative, the headquarters of which are housed in the 17th-century Château
du Bois de la Salle, where visitors can taste the wines.

CHENAS

Coming out of Juliénas travelling south, turn right onto the
D17. At the tiny hamlet of Le Fief, follow the road right
round to the left, almost in a U-turn, onto the D68 which
skirts the steep sides of a hill on your right. At the hamlet of
Les Deschamps, the D68 turns right and leads into Chénas.

Chénas is the smallest of the Beaujolais Crus. Confusingly,
most of the vineyards in Chénas are labelled as Moulin-à-Vent,
while the neighbouring village of La Chapelle-de-Guinchay
produces twice as much Chénas wines as Chénas itself.

The name Chénas comes from *chêne*, oak, because there
used to be a large forest of oak trees here. The trees, however, were cut down centuries ago. Now the village consists
of a few houses in the midst of hilly vineyards. The Château
de Chénas, not so attractive from the outside, has impressive,
arched cellars used by the local cooperative.

As a wine Chénas is closely akin to its neighbour Moulin-
à-Vent – substance and strength are its characteristics, and it
benefits from a few years' ageing. Locally Chénas is
described as 'a bouquet of flowers in a basket of velvet'.

MOULIN-A-VENT

If, instead of following the D68 round to the right, you continue straight on at the crossroads just south of the village of Chénas, shortly after you will arrive in the Moulin-à-Vent district.

The Cru Moulin-à-Vent is named after an ancient, 13th-century vaneless grain mill. It is imposingly situated on a hill between the villages of Romanèche-Thorins (the municipality to which it belongs) and Chénas on the D266. Close to the monument are the official wine-tasting rooms of Moulin-à-Vent and a few wine estates. Nowadays the view from the mill reveals a sea of grape-vines. This has not always been the case, because historically grain was grown all around the village of Romanèche-Thorins. In fact, the name Romanèche comes from Romana Esca: grain depot of the Roman legions.

The appellation Moulin-à-Vent encompasses the municipality of Romanèche-Thorins as well as approximately three-quarters of Chénas. The wine is among the best of Beaujolais, thanks to its dark colour, robust, generous soft fruity flavours and a sufficient level of tannin to allow it to mature for a few years.

The Musée Guillon in Romanèche-Thorins is interesting to visit. It houses a collection of about 100 models of wooden towers which were made by the French guild of carpenters (Compagnons Charpentiers du Tour de France). On the square, by the large church, there is a bust of Benoît Raclet (1780–1844) who, in the first half of the last century discovered a remedy for the *pyrale*, a small worm which destroys vine leaves. As the saviour of the vineyard, Raclet is annually honoured during the Fête Raclet which takes place on the last Saturday of October. The house in which he lived is now a museum.

Domaine Jean-Pierre Margerand
Good Juliénas which ages well.
Jean-Marc Monnet Excellent Juliénas: soft blackcurrant and red fruit flavours.
Michel Tête Top estate: good Cuvée Prestige Domaine du Clos du Fief.

CHENAS

RESTAURANT

Robin/Relais des Grands Crus
Tel: 85 36 72 67
One of the best restaurants in Beaujolais. The *salade Beaujolaise and poulet de Bresse rôti au four* are worth a detour. Menus start at about FF200.

RECOMMENDED PRODUCERS

Château Bonnet (La Chapelle-de-Guinchay) Château and park and firm, fruity Chénas.
Domaine des Brureaux Chénas needing three years' ageing or longer.
Domaine Champagnon Outstanding wines; dark, meaty, juicy Chénas

MOULIN-A-VENT

HOTEL

Les Maritonnes
Tel: 85 35 51 70
Stylish rooms from FF400. Restaurant is also good. Menus from FF200.

RESTAURANT

La Maison Blanche
Tel: 85 35 50 53
Cosy restaurant on the N6, where you can eat well for reasonable prices. Menus begin under FF100.

Above *The famous landmark from which the name of the village Moulin à Vent is derived.*
Right *Tradition and modern technology combined at Georges Duboeuf, in Romanèche-Thorins.*

RECOMMENDED PRODUCERS

Domaine de la Bruyère Masterful, fruity, concentrated Moulin-à-Vent.
Georges Duboeuf Since 1964 Duboeuf has worked his way up from paid bottler to biggest Beaujolais *négociant*. Now often called 'pope', 'king' or 'emperor' of this region. Fruitiness is a characteristic of all his wines.
Château des Jacques Perfectly maintained estate with strong Moulin-à-Vent and superior white Beaujolais.
Jacky Janodet Wines to lay down.
Jean Mortet Oak-matured, strong, fruity wines: best is Les Rouchaux.
Château du Moulin-à-Vent Fine, generous, quality Moulin-à-Vent.

PLACES OF INTEREST

There is a Touroparc amusement park near Romanèche-Thorins which has a zoo, a swimming pool, roller coaster, miniature train, and even a cave-boat trip.

FLEURIE

Fleurie lies directly west of Romanèche-Thorins. If you drive south out of Romanèche on the D86 you can turn right onto the D32 which will lead you straight into Fleurie. Or, from Chénas, drive south on the D68, a beautiful road with a wonderful view of the village as you approach it.

Fleurie is a peaceful village. Life centres on the square with its stores, cafés and restaurants. One shop, La Cave Vigneronne, sells wines. There is a market here on Saturdays.

On the first weekend after November 1 (All Saints' Day), the peacefulness which reigns for most of the year gives way to hustle and bustle when a large wine fair is held here with wines from Beaujolais, Mâconnais and Chalonnais: Fleurie is then invaded by thousands of winegrowers, wine-lovers and wine merchants.

Fleurie, the wine, is one of the best-selling Beaujolais Crus. A good one has lively, fresh fruitiness, with an elegant firmness and a seductive aroma of red fruits and spring flowers.

CHIROUBLES

Leave Fleurie on the D68 travelling south. After about two kilometres there is a turning to the right onto the D119 to Chiroubles. Do not turn off this road, but follow it as it climbs the hillside with the village visible on the slopes to the left. The road continues up the hill and turns almost through 180 degrees at the top. At the crossroads, turn left onto the D86 and descend towards the village.

This small village – home to the Cru of the same name – is situated at a height of 400 metres. Here the southeast-facing vineyards with granite-based soils give a light, tender Beaujolais which is usually best to drink within a year of bottling.

The village has a small, 19th-century domed church and next to it is a bust of Victor Pulliat, the brilliant researcher who found a remedy against the gluttonous grape aphid Phylloxera: by grafting onto American rootstock. The local cooperative – with tasting-room – is close by. There is also a tasting-room in a chalet on the hillside high above the village, La Terrasse du Beaujolais, where you can taste many wines from the area and eat well in the restaurant with its superb panoramic view.

MORGON

The vineyards of the Morgon Cru lie within the commune of Villié-Morgon. To reach the village of Villié-Morgon you must drive out of Chiroubles heading south on the D86 which takes you straight there.

The villages of Villié and Morgon became one municipality in 1867. Since then the border has been situated at

FLEURIE

HOTEL

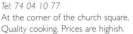

Les Grands Vins
Tel: 74 69 81 43
Modern hotel: 20 peaceful rooms
(starting at about FF350).

RESTAURANT

Auberge du Cep
Tel: 74 04 10 77
At the corner of the church square.
Quality cooking. Prices are highish.

RECOMMENDED PRODUCERS

Domaine Bernard Excellent Fleurie:
neither too light nor too heavy.
Domaine Chantreuil Balanced
Fleurie, beautifully rounded.
Michel Chignard Reliable, medal-
winning Fleurie Les Moriers.
Alain Coudert Relatively powerful,
fragrant Fleurie Clos de la Roilette.
Domaine de la Grand' Cour
Fruity, juicy Fleurie with firm backbone.

CHIROUBLES

RESTAURANT

Chez Marc et Annick
Tel: 74 04 24 87
Cosy inn in the centre of the village. For
less than FF100 you can eat very well.

RECOMMENDED PRODUCERS

Domaine Bouillard Distinctive,
lively, elegant wine. Drink within a year.
Domaine Cheysson-les-Farges
Well made, distinctive Chiroubles – a
frequent award winner.
Domaine de la Combe aux Loups
Aromatic wines, complex and lengthy.
Bernard Méziat Sturdy, fruity wines.
**Alain Passot/Domaine de la
Grosse Pierre** Fresh, fruity
Chiroubles – delicious when young.
Francis Tomatis & Fils Family
estate for excellent Chiroubles listed
at some of France's best restaurants.

MORGON

HOTEL

Le Villon
Tel: 74 69 16 16
Hotel with 45 spacious rooms (start-
ing at about FF375). It serves various
Morgons with regional dishes.

Left Landscape of Fleurie, one of the most popular Beaujolais Crus, noted for wine with delicious fresh fruitiness.

Above and Right *Aspects of life in the Beaujolais region: harvesting, barrel-cleaning, and inevitably beautiful surroundings.*

RECOMMENDED PRODUCERS

Domaine de la Chanaise Leading property; powerfully bouqueted Morgon.
Louis Claude Desvignes Morgons with good fruit and rich tannins.
Domaine des Pillets Well-made Morgon needing two years' ageing.
Domaine Pierre Savoye Attractive Morgon Côte du Py with intense colour and flavour, and good suppleness.

BROUILLY

HOTELS

Le Mont Brouilly
Tel: 74 04 33 73 (Quincié)
30 rooms (about FF300), peaceful at rear with a view of Mont Brouilly.

RESTAURANTS

Monique et Jean-Paul Crozier
Tel: 74 66 82 79 (St-Lager)
Welcoming, unpretentious; good for wholesome food. It is also has a bar.
Christian Mabeau
Tel: 74 03 41 79 (Odenas)
The best restaurant of both the Crus.

RECOMMENDED PRODUCERS

Domaine Ruet (Cercié) Usually exquisite wine: lively and full of fruit.
Bernard Champier (Odenas) Tiny estate for strikingly good Brouilly.
Château Thivin (Odenas) Excellent Côte de Brouilly and Brouilly.
Laurent Martray (St-Etienne-la-Varenne) Be sure to try the Brouilly Cuvée Vieilles Vignes.

Mont du Py, the 352-metre high remains of a volcano, with Villié on the north side of the hill and Morgon on the south side. Mont du Py and Charmes are two of the best vineyards of the Morgon appellation. Underlying schistous rock helps produce a substantial, generous wine. In fact, it has been said of Morgon's wine that it has: '*Le fruit d'un Beaujolais, le charme d'un Bourgogne*'. A classic Morgon is distinguished by its aroma of wild cherries and there is frequently a substantial core of alcohol.

Morgon's wine tasting room is one of the most visited of the region. It is housed in the arched cellars of a castle near to the village centre.

BROUILLY AND COTE DE BROUILLY

From Villié-Morgon, follow the D68 south towards the Côte de Brouilly and the village of Brouilly itself.

The entrance to southern Beaujolais is dominated by the 483-metre Mont Brouilly, an extinct volcano. The vineyards growing on its slopes have their own appellation, that of the Cru Côte de Brouilly. Wines from this appellation are usually large, mouthfilling and light in alcohol thanks to the optimum levels of sun which hit these hillside slopes. At the same time, the wines have a refined aroma, often with hints of violets and raspberries.

The vineyards surrounding the volcano belong to the Brouilly appellation which has the biggest yield of all the Beaujolais Crus. The appellation is made up of parts of the communes of Cercié, Charentay, Odenas, Quincié-en-Beaujolais, Saint-Etienne-la-Varenne and St-Lager. Differences in the soil and the large number of producers mean that there are many styles of Brouilly, but fruit and firmness are the prevalent characteristics.

All the villages of Côte de Brouilly and Brouilly have their own charm. Follow the D68 to Cercié with its ancient chapel. Then travel on to Saint-Lager where you will find several small châteaux and the Cuvage des Brouilly (the tasting room of both Crus). At Saint-Lager, the D68 splits in two, with the D68E continuing straight on and the D68 turning left. Take the latter road, turning left after about one kilometre (still the D68) to Charentay. Here you can see the ruins of the castle of Arigny and (along the road to Odenas) the 19th-century Tour de Belle-Mère.

Close to the village of Odenas are two castles: the 17th-century Château de Pierreux to the north and the much grander Château de la Chaize to the west.

If you drive south out of Odenas on the D62 you will come to Saint-Etienne-la-Varenne, a picturesque village built in terraces which is pleasant to stroll around.

Quincié-en-Beaujolais is situated northwest of the Mont Brouilly on the D9. Here there is a cream-coloured church, a large cooperative and the imposing 15th-century castle of Varennes (along the road to Marchampt).

REGNIE

In 1988 the nine existing Beaujolais Crus were joined by a tenth, Regnié, lying west of Morgon and Brouilly. The wine is colourful, expressive, very fruity and fairly firm. To get to there from Odenas, take the D43 heading north, turn left onto the D37 and then, after one kilometre, turn right onto the D9 which takes you into the village.

The most impressive building in Régnié-Durette is the church with two tall towers and nearby is the local tasting - room. Outside the centre lies the striking Domaine de la Grange-Charton belonging to the Hospices de Beaujeu: it is an enormous courtyard, surrounded by houses and cellars. It has an immense underground vaulted cellar. There are two castles near the village: Châteaux de la Pierre and des Vergers.

REGNIE

RESTAURANTS

Auberge la Vigneronne
Tel: 74 04 35 95
Rustic, inexpensive country restaurant.

RECOMMENDED PRODUCERS

Desplace Frères/Domaine du Crêt des Bruyères Pure Régnié with good fruit; has won many awards.
Domaine de la Gérarde Firm Regnié with a pleasing amount of fruit.
Domaine Passot les Rampaux Good Regnié and a Morgon.
J-P Rampon Lively, elegant Regnié.

SOUTHERN BEAUJOLAIS

The southern part of Beaujolais consists of both flat and pronouncedly hilly areas. The wines produced here are given the appellations Beaujolais-Villages and ordinary Beaujolais (in red, white and rosé), but, apart from wine, the region has a lot to offer the tourist. It is worth the effort of exploring this beautifully varied and unspoilt countryside with its attractive golden-stone *(pierres dorées)* villages by the following route.

It begins with a short excursion to Beaujeu, which is to the west of the Côte de Brouilly, along the D37 road. The centre consists of a long street, which runs past the church of Saint-Nicolas (a good place to park). Nearby you will find the tasting room of Beaujolais-Villages: the Temple of Bacchus. Next to it is the town hall, which houses the Syndicat d'Initiative (Tourist Office) and the Musée des Arts et Traditions Populaires. Across from the church there is a pretty half-timbered building which now serves as the Maison du Pays de Beaujeu et Haut-Beaujolais – an exhibition space and a shop.

Returning east along the D37 from Beaujeu, and turning south onto the D43 road, you come to the village of Odenas (see page 128) and, further along the same road, you arrive at Saint-Etienne-des-Ouillières with its 19th-century Château de Lacarelle, which is the largest wine estate of Beaujolais.

Take the D62 west out of Saint-Etienne-des-Ouilliéres and, at the crossroads, turn left onto the D133 to Le Perréon where you can taste wine in the cellars of the Château des Loges (also a hotel-restaurant). Just south of Le Perréon is the village of Vaux-en-Beaujolais, on the D49. This charming hill-top village was the backdrop for the novel

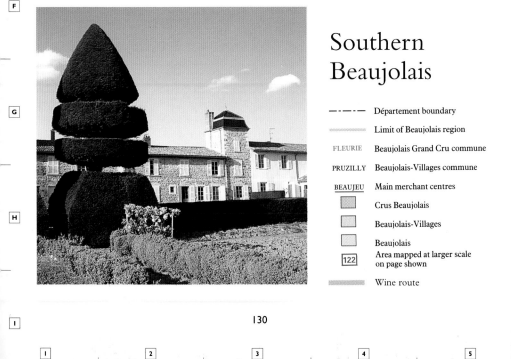

Below The grand architecture and grounds of the 19th-century Château Lacarelle, the largest wine estate in Beaujolais.

Southern Beaujolais

— · — · —	Département boundary
	Limit of Beaujolais region
FLEURIE	Beaujolais Grand Cru commune
PRUZILLY	Beaujolais-Villages commune
BEAUJEU	Main merchant centres
	Crus Beaujolais
	Beaujolais-Villages
	Beaujolais
122	Area mapped at larger scale on page shown
	Wine route

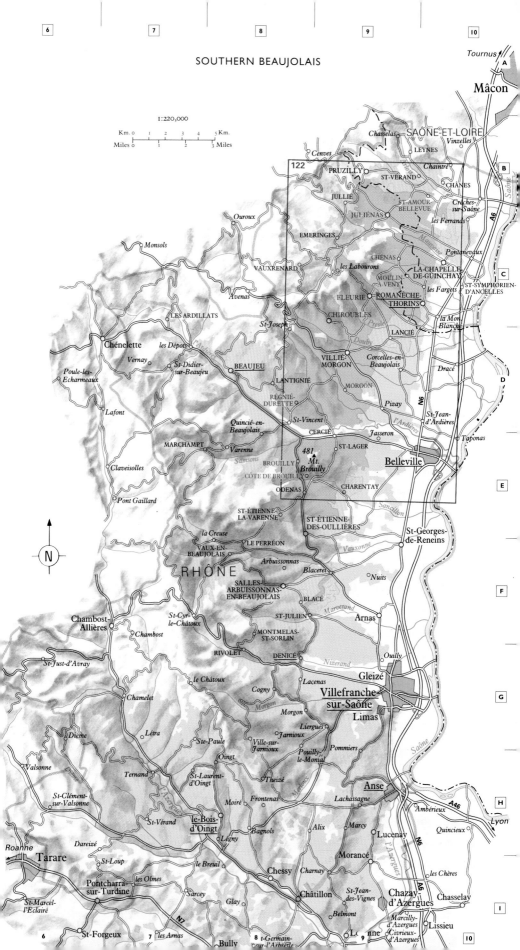

1:220,000

Km. 0   1   2   3   4   5 Km.
Miles 0   1   2   3 Miles

Tournus
Mâcon
SAÔNE-ET-LOIRE

122

Chasselas
Vinzelles
LEYNES
Cenves
PRUZILLY
ST-VÉRAND
Chaintré
CHÂNES
JULLIÉ
ST-AMOUR-
BELLEVUE
Croches-
sur-Saône
JULIÉNAS
les Ferrands
Ouroux
EMERINGES
Pontanevaux
CHÉNAS
les Labourons
MOULIN-
À-VENT
LA-CHAPELLE-
DE-GUINCHAY
ST-SYMPHORIEN-
D'ANCELLES
VAUXRENARD
les Fargets
FLEURIE
ROMANÈCHE-
THORINS
Avenas
CHIROUBLES
la Mon
Blanche
LES ARDILLATS
St-Joseph
LANCIÉ
Monsols
les Dépôts
BEAUJEU
VILLIÉ-
MORGON
Corcelles-en-
Beaujolais
Chénelette
Vernay
St-Didier-
sur-Beaujeu
LANTIGNIÉ
MORGON
Dracé
RÉGNIÉ-
DURETTE
Poule-les-
Écharmeaux
Pizay
ST-JEAN-
D'ARDIÈRES
Lafont
Quincié-en-
Beaujolais
St-Vincent
CERCIÉ
Jasseron
l'Ardière
MARCHAMPT
Varenne
ST-LAGER
Taponas
Claveisolles
481
Mt.
Brouilly
BROUILLY
CÔTE DE BROUILLY
Belleville
Pont Gaillard
ODENAS
CHARENTAY
RHÔNE
ST-ÉTIENNE-
LA-VARENNE
ST-ÉTIENNE-
DES-OULLIÈRES
St-Georges-
de-Reneins
la Creuse
VAUX-EN-
BEAUJOLAIS
LE PERRÉON
N
Arbuissonnas
Blaceret
Nuits
SALLES
ARBUISSONNAS-
EN-BEAUJOLAIS
BLACÉ
Chambost-
Allières
Chambost
St-Cyr-
le-Châtoux
ST-JULIEN
Arnas
MONTMELAS-
ST-SORLIN
St-Just-d'Avray
RIVOLET
DENICÉ
Ouilly
le Châtoux
Lacenas
Gleizé
Chamelet
Cogny
Villefranche-
sur-Saône
Dieme
Morgon
Liergues
Limas
Létra
Jarnioux
Ste-Paule
Ville-sur-
Jarnioux
Oingt
Pouilly-
le-Monial
Pommiers
Valsonne
St-Laurent-
d'Oingt
Theizé
Ternand
Anse
St-Clément-
sur-Valsonne
Moiré
Frontenas
Lachassagne
Ambérieux
Lyon
St-Vérand
le-Bois-
d'Oingt
Bagnols
Alix
Marcy
Lucenay
Quincieux
Dareizé
Légny
Roanne
les Chères
Tarare
St-Loup
le Breuil
Chessy
Charnay
Morancé
CHAZAY
D'AZERGUES
Chasselay
Pontcharra-
sur-Turdine
les Olmes
Châtillon
St-Jean-
des-Vignes
St-Marcel-
l'Éclairé
Sarcey
Glay
Belmont
Marcilly-
d'Azergues
Lissieu
N7
les Arnas
St-Forgeux
Bully
t-Germain-
sur-l'Arbresle
Civrieux-
d'Azergues

SOUTHERN BEAUJOLAIS

HOTELS

Château des Loges
Le Perréon (near Vaux-en-Beaujolais).
Tel: 74 03 27 12
Small castle hotel (10 rooms, about
FF350). Adequate rooms with rather
modern furnishings. Also a restaurant.

Hostellerie St-Vincent
Tel: 74 67 55 50 (Salles-Arbuissonnas)
This hotel has a park, swimming pool
and tennis court. The rooms are
comfortable (starting at about FF300)
and you can eat well here: *confit de
canard maison, suprême de caille*, etc.
Menus start at around FF140.

Le St-Romain
Tel: 74 60 24 46 (Anse)
Pleasant hotel with some 25 rooms
(starting at approximately FF200).
Decorated classically, but with
modern facilities. Peacefully situated a
few kilometres from the exit of the
autoroute. It also has a restaurant.

RESTAURANTS

Anne de Beaujeu
Tel: 74 04 87 58 (Beaujeu)
Tasty regional cooking (*poulet de
Bresse à la crème légère*). The most
inexpensive menu – with the speciality
of the day – costs less than FF125.
There are also seven hotel rooms,
with variable bathroom facilities. There
is a car park in front and a larger one
60 metres further up the road.

Above *Vaux-en-Beaujolais, setting
of the famous novel,* Clochemerle.
Right *Vines around the town of
Vaux-en-Beaujolais.*
Far right *Cloisters in southern
Beaujolais.*

Clochemerle by Gabriel Chevallier. Near the village church is
the subject of Chevallier's book: a urinal, and you will find
another one near the Musée Viticole et Agricole (in a side
street next to the church). Black, metal signs point out the
way to shops and craftsmen in Vaux.

From Vaux travel along the D35 road southeast. This is a
marvellous, winding road to Salles-Arbuissonas, along the
way there are some spectacular views over the surrounding
countryside. In the village, park near the town hall and walk
under a gateway to the church and the 10th-century
monastery, founded by the monks of Cluny. There are wonderful frescos in the chapter house and next to the church is
a fine, peaceful cloister.

To the east of Salles, Blaceret has a good restaurant serving regional dishes. Also worth visiting are Blacé with its
19th-century castle (follow the D19), also, the village of
Cogny, again on the D19, where the church is built from
the ochre-coloured *pierres dorées* so characteristic of southern
Beaujolais. Lierques is the next stop. This little village has an
good wine cooperative as well as an interesting church
to see, with frescos and stone statuettes of craftsmen and
winegrowers decorating the walls.

Then on to Pommiers. Drive east out of Cogny on the
D84. Turn right at the crossroads onto the D76 and
continue until you reach the D38. Turn right onto the D38,
travelling south for about two kilometres and then turn left
and left again to reach the village of Pommiers where, in the
15th-century church, there are curious stone animal heads
to be seen.

Now drive south on the D70, turning left after one kilometre to Anse, which has Roman mosaics in the Château de
Tours. Then, stopping briefly at Lachassagne on the D39,
for the view and the art gallery La Cuvée, go back onto the
D70 to Charnay.

Above *A house with vines in Oingt, a beautiful little town dating from the medieval period.*
Below *View over the village of Jarnioux.*

Auberge de Clochemerle
Tel: 74 03 20 16 (Vaux-en-Beaujolais)
Rural inn with regional specialities (terrines, *coq au vin*), fresh fish and a few surprises. Menus start at FF100.

Auberge de Liergues
Tel: 74 68 02 02
Large portions, keen prices (menus begin under FF100) at a café on the church square. Cuisine is mainly regional.

Restaurant du Beaujolais
Tel: 74 67 54 75 (Blaceret)
An ivy-covered restaurant with terrace. Many attractive dishes. A *pot au feu* is usually on the menu one day a week. Menus start at about FF130.

Le Donjon
Tel: 74 71 20 24 (Oingt)
Pleasant restaurant with a terrace and fine views. Rural dishes such as *confit de canard*. Menus start around. FF100.

Le Savigny
Tel: 74 67 52 07 (Blacé)
Stylish, classic, delicious cuisine. Menus start at about FF150. It is also a small hotel (nine rooms starting at FF300).

La Terrasse des Beaujolais
Tel: 74 65 05 27 (Buisante)
Dining room with magnificent view.

PLACES OF INTEREST

There is a golf club near Lucenay, a village slightly south of Anse. Called Le Golf du Beaujolais it has two courses of nine and 18 holes respectively.

RECOMMENDED PRODUCERS

Louis et Hélène Deschamps
Elegant Beaujolais with plenty of fruit and exhilarating freshness.

Paul Gauthier (Blacé) Ordinary Beaujolais-Villages and Beaujolais as well as the primeur versions have a lot of fruit and a pure, balanced taste.

Georges Texier & Fils (Blacé)
Attractive Beaujolais-Villages.

There are 'golden stones' galore here, as well as a church (with a giant, multicoloured statue of Saint-Christophe) and a château (also the town hall).

From here the D70E, a beautiful road, runs south down to Châtillon-d'Azarques, which is dominated by its large château with interesting wall paintings in one of its chapels. Now travel northwest, along the D485 to the fortified vil-

Left *A vine-covered outbuilding in Jarnioux reflects the timeless, rustic peacefulness of Beaujolais.*

La Folie (Blaceret) Good reputation for fruity Brouilly.
Gobet (Blaceret) *Négociant* with various qualities of Beaujolais. One of the best is Domaine des Grandes Tours.
Charmet (Le Breuil) Prize-winning wines. Red Beaujolais Cuvée la Centenaire is one of the best in the district with excellent fruitiness and flawless quality. Also very good white.
Les Vins Mathelin (Châtillon-d'Azergues) Reliable négociant with delicious, supple, fruity wines. The best are labelled with their estate names.
Cave Coopérative (Liergues) Good cooperative with modern equipment for delicious Beaujolais. The white is also worth tasting,.
Château des Loges (Le Perréon) Label for good Beaujolais-Villages wines made by the local cooperative.
René et Christian Miolane (Salles-Arbuissonas) Large estate exclusively for Beaujolais-Villages, usually of excellent quality, style, depth, fruit and refinement. There is also a small wine museum here.
Château de Lacarelle (St-Etienne-des-Ouillières) The largest Beaujolais estate and one of the oldest. Much Beaujolais Nouveau. The ordinary Beaujolais-Villages is generally lively and fruity.

lage of Le Breuil. Turn right, a little further on, to Le Bois d'Oingt, the 'city of roses', and then take the beautiful D120 northwest to medieval Oingt. One of the best ways to appreciate this charming little place is to climb the central tower in the village and enjoy the marvellous view.

To round off the tour of Beaujolais take the D96 southwest again and turn right onto the D485 to the ancient hill-top village of Ternand. The archbishops of Lyon once had their summer residences here and there are frescos from the Carolingian era in the crypt of the 15th-century church.

At this point you have reached the southernmost fringes of Beaujolais, and the great tour of the Burgundy is complete.

GAZETTEER

INDEX

Indexer's note: Names of vineyards and wines are often the same and are indexed together e.g. Bonnes Mares 44, 46 where 44 refers to vineyard and 46 to wine. Towns are given in brackets for hotels and restaurants.

PICTURE CREDITS

Front cover **Robert Harding Picture Library/ Explorer**
Back cover **Scope/Jacques Guillard**

Jason Lowe 9, 11, 16/17 centre, 17 top right, 21 top, 22, 24, 28 top, 36 centre right, 55 top right, 55 top left, 59 top right, 66 bottom, 73 right, 80/81 top, 84 top, 88, 91 right, 94, 99 100 bottom left,, 102 bottom, 107, 112 top, 114, 116 bottom, 118, 119, 121 top, 125 bottom left, 129 bottom, 130, 132 top, 133, 134 top left.
Reed International Books Ltd/Joe Cornish 5 centre top, 5 top, 16/17 top, 16 bottom, 33 centre, 42 centre, 57, 58/59, 65, 66 top, 68 bottom, 69, 89, 97 bottom.
Scope/Jean Luc Barde 12 bottom, 12/13 top, 13 bottom, 14/15 bottom, 32/33, 34, 36 bottom left, 39, 40, 42/43, 49, 51, 52, 53 top right, 54/55 bottom, 62 centre, 63 centre, 68 top, ,76, 77, 85 bottom, 86, 90/91, 92/93, 96/97, 98, 100/101 bottom, 101 top, 102 top, 103, 104/105, 108/109, 109 bottom, 110/111, 111 bottom, 112 bottom, 113, 114/115 bottom, 117, 120/121, 122, 124, 125 bottom right, 126, 127, 128, 129 top right, 129 top left, 132 bottom, 134 bottom, 134/135 top right./**Jacques Guillard** 2, 3, 5 bottom, 7, 8/9, 13 centre, 14 bottom, 14/15 top, 15 top, 20/21, 25, 26/27, 28/29 bottom, 30, 31, 36 bottom right, 36 centre left, 37, 38/39, 45, 46 top left, 46/47 top, 47 top right, 50, 53 top left, 56, 60, 62/63, 70/71, 72, 73 left, 74/75, 78/79, 80 centre, 83, 84 bottom, 85 centre, 87, 105 top right, 116 top./ **Michel Guillard** 18/19, 95, /**Jacques Sierpinski** 108 left.